WHAT'S *YOUR* FATE?

JIM PRIEST & REGGIE WHITTEN

🌓 dustjacket

www.dustjacket.com

Table of Contents

INTRODUCTION

What's *YOUR* Fate?

The brick mailbox exploded when the motorcycle hit it straight on. The young man on board was thrown headlong and lay unmoving in the grass. Bricks littered the quiet residential street about ten miles from where I was sitting in my law office on the afternoon of February 15, 2002. Then I received a phone call from Roxanne Fitzgerald. Rox was and is the administrative assistant for one of my best friends, fellow lawyer Reggie Whitten.

"Jim, Reg just called and said Brandon (Reggie's son) has been in a bad accident. He's on the way to the hospital; can you meet him there?" It took just a couple seconds for my mind to absorb the news and the request. "Sure, I'll go right up there."

I hung up the phone and began to turn off my computer when my phone rang a second time. This time it was Reg. "Jimmy, Brandon's been involved in a terrible wreck, and they took him to the hospital. Can you meet me up there?"

"Sure Reg, I'm on my way." With that I flew out the door and up to the hospital.

I met Reg Whitten 22 years earlier when we were both young lawyers trying to build a career and make a name for ourselves. Our first case together was an insignificant civil litigation matter, and we met as co-counsel in the courthouse on a routine motion. We liked each other immediately, even though he had grown up and gone to law school in Oklahoma, and I was an imported Yankee from Upstate New York. Reg told me later he commented to someone after we first met, "I like that guy. He's a smart aleck just like me."

As I drove to the hospital, I thought about and prayed for Brandon and Reg. I knew how close he and Reg were. I had no idea what had happened in the accident—or all the things that had led up to it. I prayed they would both be all right.

When I walked into the waiting area of the Emergency Room, I saw Reg kneeling down next to a young man about Brandon's age who was sitting in a waiting room chair. The young man was crying hard, and Reg had his arm around him and was trying to comfort him. I thought, *here's a man who needs comfort who instead is giving comfort to someone else.* That scene embedded itself in my memory. I waited a few moments at a respectful distance until Reg finished talking with the young man. Then he got up and turned my way. "He's gone Jimmy. He died on the way here." His eyes were red, but his voice was amazingly calm and steady.

In the days that followed, I tried to be some help and comfort as Reg walked through all the "business" things that must be done when a loved one passes away. I made phone calls to friends and tried to take some of the responsibilities off Reg, as did other friends and Roxanne. Reg didn't have a church home, and he knew I was a part time pastor, so he asked if I would handle Brandon's funeral, including preaching at the service and the graveside. We held the funeral at the church where I served, and the 900 seat auditorium was filled to overflowing. I'd like to say it was a beautiful service, and if funeral services for young people can be beautiful, I guess it was. But inside I felt a hollow sadness, and I knew Reg felt that same way only far more profoundly.

I had no idea how this time would mark a decisive, pivotal point in Reg's life. And later in mine. Reg had always been a hard charging, fun loving, smart and effective lawyer. For quite a while after Brandon's death, the wind went completely out of his sails. Later in this book, Reg will relate that part of the story and how he found his voice again. I can only say from my limited vantage point his journey has been remarkable and life changing—for Reg, those around him, and the many lives he has touched and continues to impact.

I must confess I do not like but have been impressed by A. W Tozer's memorable quote: "It is doubtful whether God can use a man greatly until first He wounds him deeply." I don't like the idea of God "wounding" anyone. But as a Christian counselor once told me, "You don't want anyone to be wounded without purpose. But sometimes, it is necessary to wound in order to heal. The surgeon wounds, but he wounds in order to heal." Maybe that's what Tozer was trying to say.

I'm not saying God wounded Reg Whitten in order to use him greatly in the lives of other people. I'm not saying God's plan was for Brandon to die. I don't believe that at all. Brandon's death was the result of a combination of bad choices and addictive genetics. But I do believe Reggie's wounds have empowered him to be used greatly by God. My friend Reg might not say it or see it that way, but I do.

The title of this book is the same question Reggie and I ask wherever we go when we speak on the topic of substance abuse: What's YOUR fate? We even have wristbands we pass out to audiences that ask that question in glow-in-the-dark letters. It's a question designed to make people think about their future. To remind them that the decisions they make today about using alcohol or other drugs will determine their fate in the future. We like asking a question better than delivering a scolding lecture. We also think it's a question our state and our nation needs to consider. The alcohol and drug related decisions made today by our private and public sector leaders will affect the fate of our state and country for many years to come. The same is certainly true for individuals of any age.

Our FATE logo (which you'll see at the bottom of the last page of each chapter in this book) communicates this message with its stylized "F" in the shape of two arrows going in different directions. The logo symbolizes the fact that the choices we make will determine our fate and we get to choose which arrow (or direction) to follow.

I trust the telling of Brandon's story, the story of FATE and learning about our own fate in the arena of substance abuse, will empower you to make smart choices about alcohol and other drugs. I also pray it will help you to be used greatly in promoting substance free living as well. May Brandon's story change your way of thinking and living as it has mine.

~ Jim Priest

This book tells stories and we believe stories can positively change lives and reduce the stigma of addiction. If you have a story of hope or encouragement about your own struggle with addiction, or a loved one's, share it by going to www.fate.org and writing it in our blog.

CHAPTER ONE
Reggie Begins His Story

Police and ambulance lights rotated all around me as I drove up on the scene of the accident. Nearby, I saw my son's pick up truck and thought to myself, *oh no, Brandon has killed some poor guy on a motorcycle.* But it was Brandon who had been on the motorcycle that ran into a brick mailbox at 60 miles an hour. One of his friends had been driving Brandon's pick up. I stopped a nearby policeman, told him who I was, and asked where my son was. "He's in the medical helicopter on his way to the hospital." But the helicopter was more hearse than ambulance that day. Brandon died before ever reaching the hospital.

It was February 15, 2002. The day was cold, but my hands were sweaty and anxiety rose in my throat as I turned on to the street where I lived. Just an hour before I had received a phone call from my twenty-five year old son, Brandon, telling me he couldn't meet me to watch the OU-OSU basketball game together as we had planned. By now, three years after learning about Brandon's addiction to prescription drugs and alcohol, I had become a walking slur detector. I could always tell when Brandon had been taking something. I interrupted his sentence. "Where are you?" I demanded.

"I'm at Chili's restaurant in Edmond. Why?" was his meek reply.

"Don't move. I'm coming to get you."

I drove like a madman to the restaurant, but Brandon had lied to me. He had become very good at lying, as are all addicts. He hadn't been at the restaurant. Instead, he had been at a bar drinking and taking prescription drugs with his friend. He was supposed to be studying for a college exam. He was supposed to be finishing up school. He was supposed to be off alcohol and drugs. But he wasn't, and when he realized he was too intoxicated to meet me that evening, he called to offer his excuses. He hadn't anticipated me demanding to know where he was or saying I was on my way to get him. He panicked and lied to me about the restaurant. Then he drove as fast as he could to get back to our house. For what reason, I'll never know.

Brandon had been drinking with a buddy that afternoon. You know the guy. There are thousands of them out there—the kind of guy who is always nearby with an invitation to join him for a drink or take a pill or smoke some pot. This was the same guy who was driving Brandon's pick up truck back from the bar, following Brandon's speeding motorcycle. He's the guy who saw Brandon hit the mailbox, saw the mailbox explode, and was sitting by the side of the road crying. He later sat in the emergency room and cried, and I tried to comfort him. He was uninjured, but he had just witnessed his friend's fatal accident.

I don't blame that guy for Brandon's death. I really don't. It wasn't the last pill and drink that killed my son; it was the first one. Brandon had become a slave to his addiction, and this guy was a not-so innocent participant in Brandon's slavery.

When I got to the hospital, they told me he'd passed away. I got to see Brandon that last time, and I just held him. I held the back of his head, and the back of his head was crushed in. There's no way I can describe to you what I was feeling. It was surreal. I thought to myself there's no way this has happened to Brandon. But it did, and it all happened just because some guy said "Take one of these" years earlier, and Brandon didn't know that he wouldn't be able to stop.

This is Brandon's story. The story of a great young man who was liked by everyone, but whose brain was constructed in such a way that addiction took hold of him, making him do things that he knew were wrong and dangerous and unhealthy. This is a story about Brandon's slavery. It's also my story: the story of a single dad who tried to be a good father but didn't know enough about the power of alcohol and other drugs; a dad whose life seemed to end when his son's did. A dad who is living proof that there is life after tragedy, and there is hope for the families of addicts.

But this is a story that is larger than Brandon's or mine. It's a story about what I have come to believe is the number one problem we face: substance abuse. In the state of Oklahoma, where I live, the annual cost of substance abuse is $7.2 billion dollars. It's hard to conceive how much money that is, but the entire budget for Oklahoma state government is $6.7 billion. If the cost of substance abuse were a tax, every man, woman, and child in Oklahoma would pay $1900 a year. In Oklahoma City, Devon Energy Corporation has built a 50 story skyscraper. It's a truly impressive— and expensive— building. You could build NINE of those Devon skyscrapers with the money we spend each year because of addiction in our state. Other states are experiencing similar numbers, as is our country as a whole.

Of course, that kind of cost is just money. We lose a lot more than money every year because of substance abuse. We really don't have a way to track how many lives are lost and ruined because of alcohol and other drugs, but the Oklahoma Department of Mental Health and Substance Abuse Services tells us substance abuse in Oklahoma causes or contributes to:

- *85 percent of all homicides,*
- *80 percent of all prison incarcerations,*
- *75 percent of all divorces,*
- *65 percent of all child abuse cases,*
- *55 percent of all domestic assaults,*
- *50 percent of all traffic fatalities,*
- *35 percent of all rapes,*
- *33 percent of all suicides.*

The death of my son Brandon is not captured in these statistics. Death certificates, at least in Oklahoma, don't show whether the death was caused or contributed to by alcohol or other drugs. Brandon's death certificate shows his cause of death as "blunt force trauma", and that is true but only partially accurate. He sustained blunt force trauma to his head as a result of the motorcycle crash, but it was really alcohol and drugs that caused the accident and killed him.

The scope of the substance abuse problem is so broad and deep it takes the effort of many people to solve it. That's one of the reasons we founded a nonprofit organization called FATE—Fighting Addiction Through Education. In our organization, we say, "Fighting addiction starts with one person, but winning the fight takes a team." We believe it will take the efforts of parents, schools, businesses, churches, students, athletes and government to change the culture of substance abuse.

www.fate.org

I write this story to offer some insights I have gained and to offer hope and encouragement to those who may be facing the same trauma I faced. It is now over ten years after Brandon's death. While the wounds are still tender, there is some healing that has taken place, and I am more committed than ever to communicating the truth about addiction. Brandon once told me, "Dad, nobody ever told me you could start doing this stuff and not stop." I want to make sure no other young person can say they weren't told. And I want to enlist the help of many people and organizations to change the culture of substance abuse in our state and our nation.

CHAPTER TWO
Life Before the Mailbox Exploded

Brandon and Reggie

I had a son born in 1976. His name was Brandon. Like sons do, he changed my life.

It's hard to tell this story, even though I've told it a thousand times to groups large and small. As I gathered pictures and books and writings about Brandon to prepare this story, I dropped one of the framed photographs of Brandon. It had glass in the frame, and when I dropped it, it smashed and scattered all over the floor. I looked around and thought this is how it is; Brandon's story is just like that broken glass…a life shattered. When someone you love dies, all you have left is stuff: pictures, newspaper clippings, letters. It's hard to put a life into words. The stuff is just paper, but the person was real.

I'm from Seminole, Oklahoma. I grew up with two brothers in a very rural, blue collar family. My dad was a used car salesman, and mom stayed at home. Before Brandon was born, I had never seen a baby. Literally, I had never seen a live baby until my son was born. I had never seen one or held one, and I really had no interest in babies.

Brandon was born three days after I turned twenty one. He was born in Norman, Oklahoma where I was attending college at the University of Oklahoma. At the hospital, they held up this little guy, and I remember Brandon was born with his eyes wide open. He had these huge black eyes and he was looking right at me. He had a shocked look on his face. I think we were both a little shocked. That's the night I found out I was pretty good with babies. So that's how our relationship got started, and my life has never been the same since.

My marriage didn't work out, so I became a single dad pretty early on. When Brandon was little, he spent a lot of time with

his mom and both sets of grandparents. We had pretty good family support. But as the years went by, Brandon spent the vast majority of his time living with me as a single father. I eventually bought a house in nearby Moore, Oklahoma, and that's where he lived most of his life.

When Brandon was old enough to walk, we noticed he wasn't walking right; he was tripping and falling more than I thought he should. Like I said, I didn't have any experience with babies, but it seemed to me he was very bowlegged and his toes were pointing wrong, which caused him

Brandon in elementary school

to trip. So I took him to the pediatrician. They ended up having to put him in corrective braces just like the ones in the movie *Forrest Gump*. The braces were very painful, and I was the only one who could rock him to sleep. He was so little he didn't understand what was going on. With those braces, he couldn't walk very well, and he sure couldn't run. So, he and I got a little taste of what it was like to have a disability.

In those early years, we never dreamed that he would grow up to be an athlete, because he sure

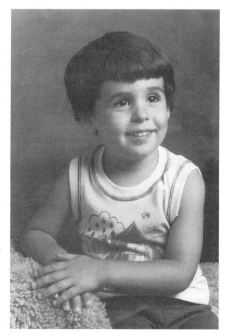

Brandon in elementary school

didn't look like an athlete in those braces. He had to wear braces for many years, but eventually his out legs straightened out. I always thought that was one reason he had such incredible strength in his legs.

A young Brandon

Bob Whitten (Reggie's dad), Reggie and Brandon

Right:
Brandon during
elementary school

Left:
Brandon during
elementary school

Left:
Reggie and Brandon

Right:
Brandon with Santa

Brandon in middle school

Top:
Brandon and his
Westmoore High
School football
teammates

Left: Brandon as
the Westmoore
High School
homecoming king

Reg and Brandon

Brandon in his Westmoore High School football

Brandon during college

Brandon, after winning the NAIA football national championship at Southwestern Oklahoma State University with his little brother Dylan and younger sister Crissy

High School and College

Brandon had a little different personality than I do. I was always really shy, but Brandon was not. He was a real people person who always had a smile on his face, a big laugh; that's why everybody kind of loved him. He was probably the most popular kid at Westmoore High, which was the biggest school in the state at the time. Brandon had a great group of friends, and I know now how important that is if you want to raise kids who are free of substance abuse. I had the privilege of watching these kids grow up, so it was really a special time in my life.

Brandon ended up being a star football player at Westmoore, and he was a very talented player. He kicked and punted, but he also played offensive line and defensive line. It seemed like he never left the field. In practice one time, he kicked a 50 yard field goal. He had an incredibly strong leg. He was a very gifted athlete, and I think he got that from his mom's side.

This is hard to talk about, but Brandon had passed that point where your kids are just your kids. Brandon had grown into something different, and our relationship had developed into something different. He wasn't just my kid anymore; he was my friend. It started out as a subtle thing, and it kind of snuck up on me when

Brandon and Reggie before Brandon's high school prom

I realized he is my friend, too. You have to have a close father-son relationship to understand that. Here's this little guy that I took care of when he was handicapped all those year, and all of sudden he's gotten big and capable of helping me and hanging with me and laughing, and so we became friends. He became independent and very skilled at many things. When he turned 18 and graduated, the idea that I had to take care of him was long gone.

In fact, he was kind of wanting to care take me. When he went to college, he was more worried about me than I was about him. We were past all of this stuff about drinking or doing drugs or breaking the law or things like that. Or so I thought. Those didn't even enter my mind at that point. This kid knew right from wrong. He'd been raised right, and I was confident he wasn't going to do any of those things. He wasn't going to break the law, and he wasn't going to do drugs. Not my kid. So I actually quit worrying about that stuff. I worried about it when he was 15, 16, 17, but not when he went off to college. I have a total of 5 kids and step-kids, and Brandon was the easiest to raise. He got in the least amount of trouble; he was

Brandon during his college years at
Southwestern Oklahoma State University

very reliable. I just didn't worry about him.

In his senior year, Brandon was recruited by a number of NCAA Division 1 colleges like Oklahoma, Oklahoma State and the University of Arkansas. He decided to go to Arkansas where he played football for a year. But he got homesick, so he came back to Oklahoma and transferred to Southwestern Oklahoma State University at Weatherford. They were a very good football team that year, and it was thrilling to watch him play. Southwestern ended up playing for the National Championship, and they won the whole thing. It was an exciting time for all of us.

The First Accident

When Brandon was in college, I thought he really had his head screwed on straight. He wanted to get his degree; he wanted to go to law school. He wanted to come back to Oklahoma City after graduation and hang with me. I figured we would practice law together, and I would show him all the stuff I know and be his mentor. I figured he'd live down the street from me and have grandkids. I thought all those things, but none of it came true.

The idea that Brandon would do drugs was ridiculous to me. There was no way, or so I thought. But I didn't know very much about addiction at that point. When I grew up in Seminole, we

First accident

didn't have drugs, at least that I knew about. We had kids drinking beer and driving around dirt roads, but nothing very serious. We heard about drugs, but alcohol was the only drug that people used when I grew up. I never imagined it would strike my son. Brandon was such an athlete I thought he wouldn't ever want to mess with that stuff. The only thing I knew about addiction was that addicts are bad people. They make bad choices. I thought addicts got what they deserve. They are just bad people doing bad things. I really thought that. I don't even know where I got that misconception. Maybe it was growing up watching Andy Griffith. Otis the town drunk always wanted to be in jail so he could get a free lunch. That's what I thought. Addicts just choose their path and deserved the results of that choice. I didn't believe it could ever happen to me or any of my kids. I know now that's wrong. Addicts don't look like Otis, and they don't always look like the guy sleeping on the street. They look like Charlie Sheen and Whitney Houston and former OSU basketball coach Sean Sutton. They look like you and they look like me. They look like my son. But I didn't know that while Brandon was alive, so I thought there was no way my son could ever be an addict.

That was my mindset while Brandon was in college. With that mindset, I was sleeping peacefully one night when a phone call interrupted and changed my life. I didn't even know Brandon had come to Oklahoma City, but he had driven to the City from Weatherford with his girlfriend. They had gone to see some friends and then out to dinner. Somewhere along the way, Brandon had taken

Brandon and his little sister Hannah

a valium and drank liquor on top of that. While they were driving back to Weatherford, his car ran off the road and that's what resulted in the phone call. It was the hospital telling me Brandon and his girlfriend were injured, and I should get there as fast as possible. My heart was beating like crazy as I raced to the hospital.

When I got there, I found out that between the two of them, Brandon was injured the most. He had injured his arm, and they thought they might have to amputate it. They said Brandon was drinking and driving. I talked to his girlfriend and her mother in the emergency room, and I remember thinking, *thank God she isn't hurt.* At least she didn't look hurt. When Brandon's car went off the road, the car landed upside down in a creek. The two of them were hanging upside down from their seatbelts causing them to ingest some of the dirty creek water. Evidently, she had ingested quite a lot of that water. When I got to her room, they had put a tube down her throat. Everybody said she was going to be fine. She couldn't talk, but she had a little blackboard and was writing me notes saying, "It's OK", and "How's Brandon?" I hadn't even seen Brandon at that point, but I was relieved that his girlfriend was going to be fine.

I turned my attention to my son, and it looked like he was hurt badly. But as the days went by, it was determined they would not need to do an amputation and he would eventually heal.

While Brandon was recuperating in the hospital, I got a chance to talk with him about what happened, and I learned that he had been taking valiums and drinking for some time. I couldn't believe it. I knew what a valium was, and I asked him, "Why in world would you take a valium? Who gave it to you?" He told me all the guys on his football team take valium in the weight room after practice. He said the players would actually carry a flask of whiskey when they got in the whirlpool and drink whiskey while taking valium. I was incredulous.

"Why would you do that?" I asked him.

"All my buddies said to do it, that it would help with the aches and pains of football. We didn't do it before practice. We did it after practice, so it was okay."

I couldn't believe it. I just couldn't believe it. Brandon was not a follower. He was not the kind of guy who would bend to peer pressure. But that's what happened. Somehow, in the context of college and a team who used drugs and alcohol, Brandon became a follower. That's the power of peer pressure.

As the days went by after the accident, Brandon's girlfriend did not get out of the hospital, and we grew more and more worried. Brandon was too hurt to visit her, and we never told him how she was doing because he was so weak. I didn't want to worry him. I always said she was doing fine, even though she was getting worse. It turned out she caught a staph infection called MRSA, which is really bad. I had never heard of MRSA before, but she got this infection in her lungs and steadily got worse and worse. We just kept praying she would get better.

But she wasn't getting better; she was getting worse. One day I got a call from her parents and her mom said, "Reggie, you need to bring Brandon up here, so he can say goodbye."

Stunned and saddened, I got Brandon out of bed, and he had to lean on me to walk. I didn't tell him until we got on the hospital floor that she was really sick. As we got off the elevator, it was a straight shot down the hallway to her ICU. I could see her lying in her bed, and when she saw us she immediately started crying. Brandon could see her too, and he started crying. As we got closer the two of them were sobbing. I really don't remember what Brandon said. All I could hear was him sobbing.

After awhile, we took Brandon out, and he kept saying, "Tell me she's going to be OK", and I said, "I don't know, son. I don't know

Brandon and Dylan

Brandon and his little brother Dylan

if she's going to make it." Sure enough, that day she died. I had to break the news to him, and he was never the same after that; it just killed him.

The aftermath of that wonderful young woman's death was terrible, I'm sure, for her family. I know it was for Brandon. He felt such guilt over her death. A few days later we loaded him into the car and went to the funeral. Her parents were just incredible people. They loved Brandon, and they had us sit with them at the funeral, which you know, it takes pretty good people to do that. They gave Brandon her favorite teddy bear that they had on the coffin, and he cried more than anybody did at the funeral. He was never the same.

I began talking to him about his addiction. "How did this happen?" "Why?" He told me he had tried to quit. But he would get nervous and anxious, and then he'd take a valium. On the night of the crash, he and his girlfriend had been in a fight. "I was all anxious, and I just felt this urge to take a valium, so I did." Of course, he also had some drinks, and now all of a sudden, it felt like I didn't even know my own son.

Here's this kid that I had known for all these years, and now he's drinking, taking drugs that don't belong to him, and driving? It was a nightmare, but I was awake, and it wouldn't end.

The night that Brandon had the car crash with his girlfriend was the first night that I ever knew he was doing anything. I didn't think he drank, I didn't think he smoked; I didn't think he did drugs. I later found out he did all those things. I don't think he'd been doing them very long. I never could pin him down on a date. Somewhere in his college years, he was introduced to the concept of drinking and taking drugs. Oddly enough, he would only smoke cigarettes while he was drinking. This was a college football player, an athlete, and we had talked about cigarettes before. He thought people who smoked cigarettes were stupid. He wouldn't do it because he was an athlete. But when he would get high, he would do stupid stuff. I think some of the things he did surprised even him. It certainly surprised me. I had no idea this was coming.

I found out this kid who was not a follower somehow in college became a follower. He gave into the power of peer pressure. His friends were telling him it's okay to do this, it's cool to do it, it's fun to do it, and he gave in.

You just have to understand this was a kid that I could always talk to, and he followed every suggestion or direction I had ever given him. He made plenty of mistakes, but when he made them, we would talk about it, and he would learn from them and do better. Because he wanted to be a lawyer, reason and rationality were a big part of his life and mine. We would talk about things he had done wrong, and he would say, "Dad I'm sorry; I'll study harder" or whatever. So the concept that he wouldn't or couldn't just stop was foreign to me. I told him if I do something that's bad or hurts, if I don't get enough sleep, if I eat too much or if I drink a little too much, I just don't do it anymore. I stop. I use willpower. That's what got me through law school and made me a successful lawyer. Brandon knew that. We talked about it. Willpower was the way to go. You have to be motivated and do what you're supposed to do. That's how he played on a national championship football team. He knew all about willpower, he knew all about practicing football, lifting weights and he was good at those things.

What I found was that willpower wasn't enough. This kid had a lot of willpower, and he could not stop. That was what he was amazed about. He was just as surprised as me. He said, "Dad, nobody told me you could get into this stuff and you couldn't get out." Brandon was not a bad person; he was a great kid, but the decision to take the first valium was really the most important decision. It wasn't the last valium that killed my son; it was the first one. It wasn't the last drink he took; it was the first one.

After the First Accident

After his girlfriend's funeral, I sent him for treatment in Arizona. Someone said he needed to go into thirty day treatment, and I thought that was a long time. I figured you could fix anything in thirty days and that Brandon would be fine when he got out. But I was wrong.

He did look and sound better when he got out of treatment. He was full of new information, and he was optimistic. He told me that when he was in therapy, the doctors told him there are genetic predispositions. Some people have it; some people don't. He said there are certain drugs to which certain people have a genetic predisposition to become addicted. Some people get addicted to nicotine. Brandon said, "I'm not addicted to nicotine. Everybody smokes when we're out in these bars. So I'd smoke, but I don't care if I ever smoke again. And alcohol, I can take it or leave it. But I've got to have these valiums. You know I get all anxious, and the only way to cure my anxiety is to take a valium, and I can't stop." He would try. He would use willpower, and he would stay clean for a long period of time. But he just couldn't seem to stop.

We began to have these peaks and valleys. He would go a long time and everything would go fine. Then I would catch him. I became a walking slur detection machine. I watched him like a hawk. I talked to him all the time, and I could tell when he was drinking and taking valiums. I could just tell. Later, I learned that recidivism is the norm; going back and forth is what most often happens. On drugs, off drugs is the norm. It's not the oddity; it's the norm. But I didn't know that.

I've got to tell you it was the wildest roller coaster I've ever been on. Between the time his girlfriend died and the time Brandon ultimately died, we were constantly going up and down. It was so frustrating, because willpower was not enough. It's like trying to protect yourself from somebody shooting off a gun by holding up a piece of paper. It's nothing. There was no way willpower was going to help. But I didn't know that. I just kept urging him, "Use willpower, do the right thing; you know what the right thing is!" He just couldn't respond.

During this time, I detected Brandon's Achilles' heel. Brandon and I were very close. For so many years it was just the two of us, and he had become very protective and afraid of disappointing me. I decided his Achilles' heel was that he didn't want to hurt me; I thought maybe I could use that. I began telling him, "Look, if you don't care about yourself, look what you're doing to me. How could you do this to me? " I thought maybe I could guilt him into quitting. I can see now, in retrospect, that was a bad idea and very ineffective.

When I would say things like that, Brandon would start crying and saying, "Dad, I'm so sorry. I'm so sorry; I won't do it again." Then, he'd do it again.

I would talk to him and say, "You promised me you would never do this again. How could you do this to me? How could you do this to you? How could you do this your baby sister? How could you do this to your baby brother? How could you do this to your family?" He would just cry. Here's a 6'3, 270 pound kid crying. He was genuinely sorry and sincere in his promise making, but he and I didn't know what it took to make the promises stick.

By Christmas 2001, Brandon was 25 and had gone 6 months without having a drink or a valium. Things were going well. Brandon seemed to be on track finishing up his college courses, and he had a new girlfriend. I got them tickets to see the Nutcracker Suite, and that's the night he weakened. I found out that Brandon had slipped out of the ballet, went downstairs, got some alcohol, and took a valium.

I guess his new girlfriend was like me, because she got to where she could tell if he'd been drinking or using from his speech pattern. So when he came back into the theatre, she busted him. She walked out, and they broke up. I was out of town at the time, and he called me crying and told me the story and, like his girlfriend, I could tell he had been taking valium and drinking. It was a black Christmas that year. When I finally got home, I was mad and I was desperate. By this time I had talked to a lot of counselors, and they said, "You are going to have to exercise tough love. If he does this again, you are going to have to tell him the consequences. He's got to go away.

Brandon with brother Dylan and sister Hannah

You've got to take that car away from him. You can't turn him loose drinking and driving."

So I sat Brandon down that last time, and I think it's the only time that Brandon ever saw me cry. I said, "If you do this again, I want you to go away. I want you to go away from your sisters. I want to go away from me, I want you to go away from your little brother, and I don't ever want to see you again, so don't do it again. Do you understand me? Don't do it again; don't make me do this."

Brandon said, "I would never hurt you again like this dad. I'm not going to do it."

Things Get Better....and Worse

Things seemed to get better. He went a month and a half completely sober. On Valentine's Day, our whole family had dinner at a friend's house, and when we were done, we walked out to the car together. He loaded his baby sister in the car seat and somebody snapped a picture of the two of us. Right after the picture was taken Brandon said to me, "This is what a family ought to be like."

He spent the night with me at my house, and he had a college exam the next day. He told me he was going to study, take the

The last photo taken of Brandon, Valentine's Day 2/14/02

test, and then that night we made plans to watch a basketball game together on TV. So I went to work, and he stayed at my house and studied.

At noon on February 15, 2002, I received a phone call from Brandon. He said, "Hey dad, I have something that came up, and I can't be there tonight to watch the game with you." And I knew. I just knew he had been using. His speech was just a little bit off. I asked him "Where are you?" He said, "I'm a Chili's restaurant in Edmond. Why, what's wrong?" I told him, "You stay right there. I'll be right there. Just wait for me right there." I hung up the phone, and that's the last time I ever talked to my son.

I slammed my phone down and a very angry me drove to Chili's in Edmond. But on the way, I decided I needed to chew his ass out some more. I was going to tell him what I was about to do. So I called him on my cell phone, but he didn't pick up. I left him a pretty angry voicemail, and I told him what I was going to do. I was going to take away his car, and I was going to make him go away just like I warned him the last time.

When I got to Chili's, Brandon's red pick up was nowhere in sight. That just made me madder. I called and called and drove around, and I couldn't find him anywhere. I decided to go to my house thinking maybe he went there. I called his mother who I hadn't talked to in years and said Brandon's had another "event". I told her what I was going to do and said, "He's gotta go away."

When I pulled in my neighborhood, I saw flashing red lights and a bunch of cars in the middle of the road. I saw the fire trucks. I didn't see the evacuation helicopter because it had already taken off. I saw Brandon's truck by the side of the road, and in front of the fire truck there was a crushed motorcycle I didn't recognize. I remember there were bricks in the road everywhere. I was still on the phone with Brandon's mother and I told her, "Oh, my God. He's hit some poor, innocent guy on a motorcycle, and he's probably killed him."

I hung up, and I ran up to the bike. The policemen saw me coming and intercepted me.

"Whoa, whoa, whoa. Who are you?"

"That's my boy's truck. Where is he?"

That's when I saw there was a young man laying in the grass by the side of the road. He was crying, and I had no idea who he was. He didn't look like he was hurt. He was just crying in the grass.

I couldn't see Brandon anywhere. The police explained that Brandon had been on the motorcycle, and the guy crying in the grass had been driving Brandon's truck. Brandon was actually at the Oak tree golf course restaurant and bar drinking with his friend. He was never at Chili's. But after he lied to me on the phone about where he was, he hung up and told his friend, "My dad's coming; we gotta get home." So they raced out of there.

Brandon and I had been avid motorcyclists forever. He was an excellent driver. But not when he was taking valium. When he left Oak tree and entered our neighborhood, he must have been going very fast. I don't know what he was thinking or what he was going to do, but he was in a terrific hurry. It's a 20 mph speed limit in that neighborhood, and they told me, going 65, he hit a brick mailbox, and it exploded.

When I got to the hospital, they told me he had passed away. I got to see him that last time. I held him, and I held the back of his head. The back of his head was crushed in. There's no way I can describe to you what I was feeling. It was surreal. There was no way this happened to Brandon. There was no way.

Then that young man walked in the room behind me—the same guy who was out there crying. I later found out he's the one that called Brandon and said, "Can I come over?" He's the one that gave Brandon the valium. This kid was totally out of control with remorse and emotions—even more than me, because I lost my mind there for a little bit. I sort of came to, and I saw this kid crying. I put my arm around him. I told him it was okay.

I know he didn't mean to hurt anyone. He was just another addict. Just like my boy. I don't know why I comforted him, and my friend Jim Priest, who saw me doing that, said he was amazed at how compassionate I was. But how could the parents of Brandon's girlfriend forgive me and Brandon? How could they have enough compassion to invite us to sit with them at the funeral? But they did. So how could I not forgive this boy?

That's when all of our lives changed: Brandon's sisters, his little brother, me, his whole extended family. It was like shockwaves got sent out. He had grandparents; he had cousins. He had all these people who loved him, and they were just as devastated.

And it all happened just because someone in a locker room said, "Take one of these", and he didn't know that he couldn't stop. None of us has been the same since. None of us ever will be the same.

Second Accident

Brandon's 25th and last birthday

WHITTEN
Brandon N. Whitten, age 25, of Edmond, passed from this life Friday, February 15, 2002. The son of Reggie Whitten and Terry Hudson, Brandon lived life to the fullest. He was deeply loved by many, and he loved his family and friends deeply as well. Brandon was a student at Oklahoma City Community College where he was studying to be an EMT/Fireman and he worked at All American Fitness Center. An outstanding football player at Westmoore High School, Brandon received letters of recruitment from numerous football programs ranging from the University of Oklahoma, Oklahoma State, and Nebraska and ultimately elected to attend Southwestern Oklahoma State. He was a member of Wildwood Community Church in Nor-

man. Brandon was a young man of great promise whose good looks and outgoing personality made him popular. But it was his deep love for people and for life that wove its way into the hearts of his friends and family. His death will be mourned by the many who will miss him, but his life will also be celebrated by the many he touched. Brandon was preceded in death by his grandfather, Robert L. Whitten and is survived by his father Reggie, mother Terri, uncles Craig Whitten of Norman and Kevin Whitten of Kansas City; sisters Hannah Whitten, Crysten Cheatwood and brother Dylan Cheatwood of Yukon; grandparents Agatha & Joe Blair of Norman and maternal grandparents James & Donna Crawford of Seminole. A memorial service will be held 11 a.m. Wednesday, February 20, 2002 at Oklahoma City First Church of the Nazarene, 4400 NW Expressway, OKC with burial at Resthaven Memorial Gardens in Seminole OK under the direction of Swearingen Funeral Home. In lieu of flowers, expressions of sympathy may be made to Positive-Tomorrows, PO Box 61190, OKC, OK 73146-1190.

Brandon's Obituary

CHAPTER THREE
After Brandon's Death

After Brandon died, for a while there, I just kind of lost my mind. I don't even remember anything after the first week. I just have fleeting memories. I remember I had to pull myself together, because I had kids.

I had to write an obituary, and I'd never written an obituary before. That was quite a task. How do you sum up somebody's life in a few paragraphs? I don't remember much about the funeral or the weeks that followed. For a while there, I was totally lost. I didn't have a clue what I was doing. I will say this: you know I am living proof that you can survive the death of a child. But it is the most difficult thing I have ever been through. There's nothing else like it. We parents are hardwired to give our lives for our children. I would have stepped in front of a bullet for Brandon. I would have stepped in front of a train. I would have done anything to save his life. When you fail to save your kid, now what? I did not want to live. I wasn't suicidal; I just didn't want to live. I quit eating. I dropped about 30 or 40 pounds. I absolutely did not want to live.

It's a strange feeling when you lose a child. I kept telling my friends, "I'm on fire." It felt just like somebody poured gasoline on me and lit me. I couldn't stop. I'd lie in bed at night, and it felt like I was on fire. My skin was on fire; my mind was racing. I couldn't sleep. I couldn't figure out what to do with my life. After a while, I went back to work and threw myself into my work with a vengeance, which had a little bit of effect. It got my mind off it a little bit, which helped, but it was only a temporary fix.

The biggest problem I had was when I went back home. Brandon had his own apartment, but he spent many nights at my house. He would often sleep over at my place, and he had this annoying habit of running down the hallway at full speed. He did it just for fun. Sometimes, I would step out of my bedroom into the hallway and he would run into me, full speed. It was like getting hit by a freight train, because he was so much bigger than me. After Brandon died, I'd be walking down that hallway, and I'd stop and brace myself thinking Brandon might be running into me. Then I'd think: *Brandon's dead. He's not going to be running into me anymore.*

Sometimes, I'd pick up my cell phone and think, *I gotta call Brandon*, and then I'd think, *I'm not calling Brandon ever again.* For a while, I would call his number just to listen to his voicemail, until they took that down.

I had to go clean his apartment out. It was indescribable, really indescribable. How can you go to your kid's apartment and pick up all their stuff and put it in a box. I kept the box in my closet in my house and called it the Brandon box. I gave away a lot of his stuff to his friends; everything that was Brandon I kept in that box. How do you put somebody's life in a box? Every time I went in my closet, I'd look in that box.

I was going nowhere fast, and I was sinking. I would put my younger kids to bed and as soon as they were in bed, the house would get so quiet it hurt. Then, I'd start feeling I was on fire. I didn't know how I'd make it through the first night, the second night, the third night. It was a nightmare. I thought I was losing my mind. I didn't know where to go, what to do. Just killing time was all I was doing. Just killing time.

I kept thinking *how am I going to raise these younger kids to where they get old enough to take care of themselves, so then maybe I can just die and quit being on fire?* It was the worst three months of my life.

Brandon was my best friend, and a big part of me died that day. You're just not hardwired to live after your child dies. I wasn't afraid of dying, and I'm still not afraid of dying. I'm afraid of living. It's the living that kills you. We're wired this way; we're just not made to live after the death of a child. Everyone who has lost a child reacts differently. I've had several friends who've lost a child and from what I've observed, most people can't talk about it. They can't, and they won't. I ultimately did something that's out of the norm. I started forcing myself to talk about Brandon to help other people. The more people I helped, the more it helped me. But not everybody is built that way.

About four months after Brandon died, something happened that changed my life in a positive way; I met a woman named Rachelle Newman. Some friends lined me up with her on a blind date, and it was like someone had given me a lifesaving drug. I went out with Rachelle that first night, and within a few minutes, I temporarily forgot about Brandon. Then when I took her home that night, as soon as I let her out of the car it was like, poof, I'm on fire again. I thought, *Oh, my God. I can't keep doing this. Now I have a new phenomenon. I'm on fire part of the time and then I'm out and then I'm on fire again.* That's what it felt like; it felt like I was on fire. Time would slow down. I didn't know what I was going to do. I got very lucky with Rachelle coming into my life though. She saved me.

Reggie and Rachelle

Helping Others Helps Me

After Brandon died a couple friends of mine talked me into going to Africa with them. Mike Hinkle and Bob Hunter were going to Uganda and they thought it would be good for me to go with them, get my mind off Brandon's death a little, and see what was going on in that civil war ravaged country. I had no interest in going and I knew nothing about Africa in general or Uganda specifically. But those guys were persistent and they finally talked me into going.

When I got over there I saw the terrible things that had happened to the children of Uganda as a result of Joseph Kony's "Lord's Resistance Army". Kony is a megalomaniac and a butcher and his LRA has been murdering, raping and kidnapping the people of Central Africa for years. I was especially shocked at what happened to the children. Children were raped, tortured, kidnapped and, seeing that, I thought to myself, I'm being selfish feeling so sorry for myself. Look at what these children have gone through. At least I'm a grown man. So to be honest with you, that Africa trip helped me get my focus off myself and to start helping the children of Uganda.

I just decided I needed to do something. How can I just sit here and watch these kids suffer? I'm suffering back home and I wish somebody would help me. But in the meantime, I've got to help these kids. And I accidentally discovered, that by helping those children, a by-product of it was that it was helping me. So we formed an organization called Pros for Africa (www.prosforafrica.com) and I became a supporter of a wonderful nun who is helping the Ugandan children.

For the last 30 years, Sister Rosemary Nyirumbe of the Sisters of the Sacred Heart of Jesus based in Juba, South Sudan, has answered the call to serve the children of northern Uganda and South Sudan. Armed with only a sewing machine, Sister Rosemary openly defied Joseph Kony and his so called Lord's Resistance Army. Since 2002, Sister Rosemary has enrolled in school more than 2,000 girls who had been previously abducted by the LRA or abandoned by their families. She teaches them to sew and make purses so they can support themselves. You can even buy some of these purses on our prosforafrica website. Helping Sister Rose has been an inspiration to me and it helped me better deal with my loss of Brandon. But I found out there were people who also needed help here in the United States.

Reggie, Sister Rosemary and Reggie's son, Jonathon

About a month after Brandon died, my teenaged daughter, Crissy, told me she had a friend that had a real struggle with drugs—a young man that she knew in school. She asked me if I would talk to him and tell him about Brandon, so I did. He was the first kid I ever talked to. I told him Brandon's story, and said I hope that you don't end up the same way my boy did.

You know what? This kid turned his life around. After I talked with him, he wrote me a letter and told me that our talk had helped him. That made me feel good, and I started thinking maybe if I could talk to people and tell them what happened to this ordinary kid named Brandon maybe that would help them.

So I began to talk to various people and tell them the story. I began to talk to schools and ultimately colleges. By now, I've lost count how many times I've told this story. When I first told it to a school, I had the hardest time not crying. Today, I go to schools all the time and I don't cry. I've worked myself into practicing to not do that just to try to tell these kids what happened. And I hope it helps.

But those words that he said haunt me: "Dad, I never knew you could do this and not be able to stop." So I tell schools when I talk to them, "I don't want you to end up like my boy. I want you to at least know before the alcohol, cigarettes, drugs, whatever; you need to know that you could become a slave."

As the years went by, I began to research addiction. In fact, I became obsessed. What killed my boy? Some of my friends told me, it's that young man that brought the valiums over; that's who killed your boy. Well, I don't agree with that. I don't think that's true. I think what killed my boy was whatever it is that causes people to get addicted. So I threw myself into studying addiction. I began to read books, magazine, scholarly articles. I talked to doctors. I talked to experts. I talked to the Commissioner of the Oklahoma Department of Mental Health and Substance Abuse Services, Terri White.

After studying for a long time, here's what I learned that I had no clue about before: our brain is a chemical machine. Why should that be so surprising? I mean, when we get scared what happens? We get adrenaline in our blood stream. It's a chemical; it's a hormone... It makes us have that "fight or flight" response. Look how powerful that is. Who hasn't been in love and felt the powerful chemistry of that? Why should we be so surprised that there are chemicals in your brain that reach out and grab a hold of you in the same fashion? They can grab you and hold you and say, "You need more of this drug."

So one of the most important things I learned from my study is that our brain is a chemical machine when you take drugs, when you drink alcohol, when you smoke cigarettes.

The "grabbing" of the brain may not have happened the first time Brandon drank or used drugs, but over time it changed his chemistry. That's what he was describing to me when he said, "I feel anxious, and I can't stop." It was because the chemistry of his brain had changed, and yes, he had become a slave.

He was a slave to that drug. Even though he was a big, powerful, strong kid with a lot of willpower, he was a slave. Now we know there are things that can be done, but it's too late for Brandon and me. My fate is to live with this. I have to live with my guilt and the poor decisions that I made. Brandon doesn't get to live with any of that. He's 6 feet under because of decisions; some of which he made and some of which I made.

I think about that word "fate" a lot. I don't think anybody's fate is cast in stone forever. I think that there is hope. That's why we started an organization called FATE, Fighting Addiction Through

Education. The purpose of that organization is to tell stories just like this.

My story is just one. There are tens of thousands of stories very similar to mine. Likewise, there are tens of thousands of stories of people who almost got killed, who got help, who had hope and were able to fight their way out. My boy just didn't make it.

There are people out there who can make it, and we want to help them. So FATE is an organization that anybody can go to for help. If you're a parent and you're going through what I went through, you can come to the FATE website, and we will help you. If you are a kid and you have a friend who's going through this, you can come to the website, and we will help you. If you are like my son Brandon and you don't know how you got into this mess and you don't know how to get out of it, you can come to our website, and we will help you. That's how FATE was created, and that's my fate—to work on this the rest of my life. That's what we're going to do.

I think Brandon would have been very proud of what we're doing. You know, when I was a little kid I got beat up on the playground sometimes. I always taught Brandon when he was growing up, "We don't pick on little kids." As he got bigger, Brandon was kind of the protector. He didn't like bullies; he liked helping people. So Brandon would have absolutely loved this. He would love what I'm doing, and he would be proud of me that I just didn't die.

I often think about what Brandon would think and what he would do. When I got down to 140 pounds, I was trying to tell myself, "What would Brandon want? Would he want me to be this miserable? Would he want me to die? Who's going to raise his siblings? He would want me to stand up and do the right thing." I used that to motivate myself a lot. There are not many days that go by that I don't grit my teeth and carry on because of Brandon.

It's funny; that's what I was asking Brandon to do. I was asking him to grit his teeth and fight this demon addiction by himself, and he didn't know how to do it. I didn't know how to do it. But we're getting smarter on this subject every day, and we can fight back.

Reggie's Story Online

CHAPTER FOUR
Ryan Eustace, Brandon's College Friend Speaks

Ryan Eustace

I met Brandon Whitten in late 1995 when he first came to Weatherford, Oklahoma for college at Southwestern Oklahoma State University. It was one of those things when I met him—it just clicked. Instant friendship. He was a great guy, and we had a mutual love of life. We liked a lot of the same stuff. It was a brother type friendship almost instantly.

Brandon was a great guy, loved life, easy going. Only thing we got in conflict about was how long it took him to get ready to do anything. And his laugh. You want to talk about a laugh that could change the atmosphere in a whole room. It was loud and boisterous, and I'd laugh because he was laughing. He had a giving soul. He would take anybody under his wing; not just financially, but he'd sit there and talk to anybody about anything whether he knew you or not. He probably got that from his dad. But he'd sit and talk with you about anything you wanted to talk about.

It's funny, but I never called him Brandon. It was always "Whitten". When Whitten and I talked about the future, we knew we wanted to be financially secure, and we wanted to have families. We wanted to do things with our kids together. We wanted to live close enough to be involved with each others' lives—have sons together and do guy stuff together. We weren't going to be just college buddies; we were going to be lifelong friends.

We were both on the football team at Southwestern Oklahoma State University, and our team ended up winning the NAIA national championship that year. Brandon was on offensive line, and I was on defense. We didn't interact very much in practice, but we got to know each other in the locker room and after practices. That's when we started drinking and using drugs together.

Brandon at the wedding of his best friend, Ryan Eustace

Drug and alcohol use in college sports is rampant, and it is everywhere. It's not a local or state problem. It's a national problem. If you play at that level, it's gonna be there, and it's going to be your decision whether or not to be the sober one. It doesn't matter how much testing they do, it still comes down to you making that personal decision.

I'm not sure when the first time we went out after practice and got drunk was or the first time we went out and smoked a joint. It just became part of our daily activities. Looking back on it now, it made no sense. By drinking and using drugs, you end up contradicting all your hard work in practice. We'd get up early for breakfast and lift weights, and then we'd go smoke a joint or take a pill between that and lunch. Here we were doing three-a-days to get our body in excellent condition and we were contradicting that at night by getting drunk.

It was work hard; then at night, unwind and party. It flowed naturally with our group. At practice it was go, go, go, so at night it was normal for us to drink five or six cocktails or smoke some marijuana before we went to bed.

It turned into us asking, "When do I have to be sober?" It didn't seem like that big of a decision at the time. It was, "Yeah, no big deal. I'll have a drink." Now, I can tell you how big a decision it was, but back then I couldn't. I wish there was a red flag with that decision or that there was someone standing there saying, "This is what this is going to lead to if you see into the future". But nobody was waving a red flag at us.

Brandon's love of life and happy attitude helped me through a lot of hard times. He was the friend that was always there for me, so much so that I ended up naming my son Whitten after him. In getting to know Brandon, I could see he and his dad had a great relationship. I don't think I ever met anyone with the admiration that Brandon had for Reggie. He was truly in awe of his dad. To hear Brandon talk about his dad was how I want my son to talk about me.

It was hard to see Brandon lie to Reggie about his drinking and drug use. When things started getting worse, I probably should've said something to Reggie. Maybe we should've said something to Reggie, and we could've nipped it in the bud.

Brandon and I moved into an apartment together that summer after our freshman year, and that's when we really started partying. We'd drink, hangout with some guys who smoked pot, do a little speed. It wasn't something we did all the time; it was an escape from reality. We thought we could party once or twice a week, but it didn't stop there. We started partying three times a week and drinking every night, and it just got progressively worse.

We had a lot of good times in the apartment before we even started partying. We talked about what we wanted to do later in life, and we always thought the same thing about everything. It was like we had a bonded, kindred spirit.

There's not a day that goes by that I don't think to myself, *I gotta tell Whitten that!* But then reality sets in that I'm not going to tell Whitten that. The hardest part of him dying is I was there when the drugs and alcohol first started. I was pretty naive in the party scene. I came from a small town in Kansas, drank a little in high school but stayed away from everything else. If I could reverse everything and do it over, I would.

It all happens quickly. First, you're just partying every once in a while. Then, you're thinking where can I get my next bag of weed or where can I get my next pill? Whatever it is you want to do. It goes from being a fun, recreational thing to an "I gotta have this" kind of thing, and it changes the way you think.

The hardest thing is to have seen it from the beginning. To know I was there from the beginning, to see his personality change, the way he spent his time—to let what was important to him be replaced by the next fun thing. I lost a friend before I really lost my friend, because he became a different guy. He didn't have control. Some of us walked away from doing that stuff, but Brandon was still there.

Did we see it coming? Was it evident? It was evident in that I was doing everything he was doing, just maybe in a smaller quantity. I might take pills on my day off—he was on them every day. Was it evident in his personality? No, he was still fun, laughing, having a good time. But there were small things that you could have picked up on. He started letting things slip. He wouldn't wash his car, and before he started drinking and doing drugs, he would've never shown up to a party with a dirty car. Stuff that was important to him before he started slipping became unimportant to him. He didn't work out like he used to.

We were all undergoing some personality changes; we were all still just kids. We weren't living on our own but for a year and a half at that point. Probably half of us were going through negative changes, not just him. Small stuff you don't see when you're standing beside it. It's like when I go to work for a week and don't see my kid. When I come back, he's taller; his teeth have come in better, stuff like that. But when I'm home 7 weeks, I don't see the changes. It was a lot of little stuff like that, that you can't see until you look back and say, wow, there was a lot of little stuff there that should've been picked up on.

We were using a lot of different types of drugs: Xanax, Valium, pain pills. Brandon didn't use pain pills as much as a lot of the guys, because he saw it as debilitating your muscles. He used Xanax, Valium, his Ritalin prescription, alcohol, cocaine, and weed. We'd go through an ounce of weed a week; don't know how many pills we took—it was a party type of deal.

I could see he was changing, and he seemed to be growing more dependent, but it was hard to confront him when we were all doing the same thing. It was probably the speed that hurt him the most. His mind would start racing. He'd feel depressed, so he'd self-medicate for that whether that was with alcohol or marijuana or the pills.

I don't think I would have called Brandon an addict when we were together in college, but he probably was addicted at that point. Addict is a funny word. Lots of people have a stereotype of an addict. Someone who is a bum, lives on the street, doesn't have a job, never takes a shower. But there's no stereotypical addict. They're walking with you every day, and you don't know it. Lots of addicts seem to function just fine much of the time. It got to where we began growing apart, because I didn't like seeing what he was doing to himself, but Brandon functioned. There's no question about his ability to function. He could put on his game face and go to class or go meet with his parents. He could cover his tracks. He had routines he went through not only in his mind but in his dress and appearance; so that he knew he could function no matter what he was on. It wasn't like you were sitting there going, "Oh man, Brandon hasn't bathed in three days." No way! Brandon was a clean dude. He spoke well, articulated well, and it seemed like he didn't have any problems. It wasn't like he had his sunglasses on inside so you couldn't see his eyes. He would look you straight in the eye no matter what he was on and not have any problem with it. He was functioning. It wasn't debilitating where he couldn't get off the couch, but underneath he was dying. It was a constant need. It was a dependency.

Brandon Meets a Girl

Brandon met a a very special girl at a party. She was going to
meet another guy, but she and Brandon instantly hit it off. She was a
blond-haired, bubbly girl—a small town girl impressed by Brandon's
car and his charm. She was constantly smiling when she was around
him. That was when everything was new and fun and easy. You don't
know all the stuff that goes along with people at that point. He
was different with her than anybody else. They spent a lot of time
together, and he opened up with her like I'd never seen him open
up with another girl. He got closer to her than he was to me, and it
was fun to watch from the sidelines as their relationship developed.
Brandon's girlfriend reined him in, which was hard because as he
became more addicted it put more strain on their relationship. She
saw the addiction as competition for their relationship. As he got
more heavily addicted, it took time away from them, and it changed
Brandon. It was hard because watching their relationship build
was fun, then towards the end they were always fighting, and most
of it stemmed from that change in Brandon. It was a change he'd
gone through while seeking that constant high. He was in need of
constant maintenance. I'm not an addiction expert to say how bad it
was, but it was constant. We always had something we were taking at
that point, whether it was his Ritalin prescription or some pills I got
or alcohol. It was always a party, and I say that like it's a good thing,
but it wasn't at that point. It was maintenance. We were always
looking for the next bag of weed, the next speed, whatever it was.

The Accident

Brandon and his girlfriend got in a car accident while driving
from Oklahoma City back to Weatherford one night. Before the
accident, they'd spent some time apart. But they had gone to
Oklahoma City to have dinner and see if they could patch things
up. The night of the accident was a time when their relationship was
on the rocks. They went out to an Italian restaurant, and he told
me later she was trying to get him to come back and step away from
doing his alcohol and drugs.

But Brandon was very persuasive. He would convince you he
didn't have any more of a problem than you have. He would say to
me, "Why are you coming down on me when you're guilty of the
same thing?" The way he talked he could make you all right with

him for the time being, and he'd convince you he was in control. He had that effect on a lot of us, and he had that effect on his girlfriend.

Apparently, Brandon had been drinking that night, and he had taken some prescription drugs because he felt stressed. On the way back to Weatherford, they were driving down Interstate 40, and he received a text or a call on his cell phone from another girl. While he and his girlfriend had been broken up, I think he'd been talking to some girls to make his girlfriend jealous, and she'd started to talk to some guys for the same reason. But they were so wrapped up in each other that there wasn't much competition. He told me later when that a call or text came in and when he tried to answer it the car took a 45 degree turn into a concrete culvert that had some standing water. The car went end over end and ended coming to rest upside down with the two of them were hanging by their seatbelts.

As a result of the accident, Brandon's arm was crushed, and he couldn't get his girlfriend's seatbelt off of her. I don't know whether he was in the car until they came and got her out or what, but he didn't even know his arm was crushed. He was so concerned with trying to get her out. But while she was hanging by her seatbelt in the creek, she ingested some of the water into her lungs. She eventually died from an infection in her lungs caused by water.

At the time of the accident, Brandon's addiction was probably at its peak, and the downward spiral had already begun. Some of us talked to him as friends saying, "It's time for you to really back off." But he saw us as hypocrites. He said, "You've done every bit of what I'm doing." He didn't see himself changing; he saw us as changing. I told him, "Yeah, I am changing. I have a 3 year old now. There's stuff I can't do." But he thought he had control. I know he did. He used to say, "I can quit if I want to quit. You quit when you wanted to, and so can I. There's no reason for me to quit or to do anything other than have fun." But the truth was he had crossed a line, and he couldn't quit. I could see that, but he couldn't.

It was hard to be part of his life at that point and see downward spiral. I got to a point where I didn't want to see him. I still loved him as a brother, and when I did see him it was good, but to know you're about to go into the pressure of, "Let's party" and have to say, "No. I can't do that because I have a kid." But it wasn't just because I had a kid. Enough is enough. I decided I wasn't going to do it anymore.

After the Accident

If he could've quit after his girlfriend died, he would have. It was tough to see him. I went to see him in the hospital the next day. He couldn't believe the state his life was in at that point. He was ready to wash his hands of it. If he could've quit on his own, he would've quit. I've never seen him hurt like he was hurting.

There was so much self-loathing. It was hard to hear him talk about himself the way he saw himself at that point. How worthless he felt, and all the potential he felt he had "pissed away". He thought he had been given so much, and he did so little with it. It was hard for me knowing what kind of person Brandon was, and then seeing how Brandon saw himself at that point. Because even through all of the bad experiences we went through, I didn't see him like that. He was still my buddy. But he didn't see himself as worthy to be breathing at that point

He felt like he'd killed his one true love. That's how he felt: she was the girl he was supposed to be with, it wasn't just some college romance. He felt like there was no way out at that point. Up to that point, he would tell you, "I can quit when I want to. You quit when you wanted to. There's just no reason for it." After his girlfriend's death, he realized he couldn't stop. That's when Brandon and his dad, Reggie, agreed it was time to get some help. Brandon ended up going to rehab in Arizona, and both he and Reggie hoped it would change the way things were.

It's funny; before rehab Brandon was dead set against smoking cigarettes, but after rehab he'd smoke a cigarette if he got a craving for doing anything. I couldn't believe he'd even say that. I don't know how he got his hatred for cigarettes, but he was adamant about cigarette smoke, but that changed after rehab.When he got finished with rehab he decided he was going to go to school to become an Emergency Medical Tech—a first responder. He felt that way he was using his life and his athleticism and strength to be a person who could save people's lives and to help people in situations that he had lived through. He was very motivated by it. It was good to see him back in that frame of mind where he saw a use for himself. This goal stemmed from his girlfriend's death, because he felt like the only way he could validate himself was to save people's lives since he had, in part, taken hers. After her death, that's the only thing that kept him going. He was going to be the person who could save someone else's life.

He moved to Oklahoma City to attend school and study, and we didn't see much each other since I was living in Weatherford. When we talked, he would tell me, "This isn't where I wanted to be." I was someplace I didn't want to be either. I'd just been divorced and was living alone; he'd been to rehab, and it was like everything had been torn away.

I talked with him about how I felt differently about all the partying, and he talked about how hard it was to let it go. All he could remember was that it was fun back when we were in college, and he wanted to be back where life was fun. I don't think he realized he was substituting those memories of fun with drug use—by being under the influence of something.

Despite all that and despite his girlfriend's death, Brandon still couldn't say, "Enough is enough." It was hard to see him lose so much and still not be able to say "Enough is enough." on his own. An addict is an addict. He couldn't walk away from it, because at that point he wanted the pills to stop the pain. At that point, it had gone from taking pills to levitate to a happy place to where he took the pills just to get out of the sorrow.

It was hard not seeing him much over the next year. I worked 50 hours a week and was going to school, and he didn't want to come back to Weatherford because of the hard memories and a lot of the same traps. But despite staying away from Weatherford and the temptations that were there, Brandon started using again. I don't know when he started using again—we didn't talk much, and he knew how I felt about it. He'd made a promise to do something with his life. He said, "I'm done with it. When I get back, I'm going to make something of my life." And I believe he had every intention of it. But he just cracked again.

When something has control over you, it takes your willpower out of the picture. He had every intention of not doing it. But when you don't have control over something and that same thing has control over you, I don't know how you get away from it. I don't know.

He wanted with every fiber of his being to be back to normal, be back in shape mentally and physically, to live a productive life. But that wasn't in the cards for him. It wasn't so much a conscious choice as an unconscious choice. I don't know if he knew what all he was losing to do it. Even if he did realize it, there was nothing he could do.

That initial choice is yours to make, whether to use or not use alcohol or drugs. Everyone says marijuana is the gateway drug, and it is, but it's also pills in your mom's medicine cabinet or alcohol at grandma's house. And that situation's going to be there, and that conscious choice is yours to either participate or not participate. To be that young is fun anyway; you don't have to be high or drunk. You can just walk away from it and not get started.

Once he got started again, Brandon just couldn't walk away.

Brandon's Death

I heard about Brandon' death from a high school buddy of his who called me. He told me that on the day Brandon died he had been talking to his dad on the phone, and Reggie could tell Brandon had been drinking or using or both and was side-stepping questions, avoiding wanting to be around him. At that point, Reggie told Brandon he was coming to get him. I guess Brandon panicked and took off on his motorcycle, and that's when he had the accident that killed him. Reggie had been there for Brandon everyday, telling him they were going to beat it. And Brandon really tried to beat it. There was no give up in either one of them.

The day Brandon died was the saddest day of my life. I truly intended to know that guy the rest of my life; not just remember him. You don't find guys like that every day. You don't find people you want to share everything with. That day when he died, and the day we buried him, it was hard to do, hard to be a part of.

Reggie asked me to speak at Brandon's funeral. It was hard to be a part of the duality of Brandon's life, which was all good times and all smiles, then to say goodbye to him, and it's nothing but sadness because of how and why it happened. It's hard to describe that duality. And then for me, who was there with him from the start of it, to address all of his family and friends—it was hard, but there was no way I would not be a part of it.

It was the most traumatic and emotional thing in my life. I'd already had a kid; I'd already been through a divorce. Neither of those events was like saying goodbye to someone you planned on knowing the rest of your life. You can't describe that loss.I don't know. There's no way to tell someone what that loss feels like if they haven't lived it. And if you haven't lived it, be grateful, because it's tough.

You live your life making all the choices you think are critical. I watch my teenage daughter get ready for school in the morning, and the most critical choice she thinks she's making is how she wears her hair. I make choices about raising my children. You choose what school you go to. But I guarantee you that not one of those choices is as critical as when you decide to do or not do drugs.

All because of that one choice. I know Reggie says it wasn't the last drink or pill that killed Brandon; it was the first one, and he's right. I can't emphasize enough that when you agree to drink or take drugs, or you stand by and let somebody else do it, you're making a life changing decision. You have to realize that this one decision is going to affect every other decision for the rest of your life. Yeah, some people can do drugs one time and be done with it, but there's no way of knowing if that's you. You have to just assume that once you ingest, inhale, shoot up, whatever, that could possibly be what kills you. And not only directly; it could kill you indirectly. It might be financially killing you, emotionally killing you, and, of course, it might literally kill you. There's no decision greater in your life than that decision to use or not use.

You're not just hurting yourself. I wish I could give every young person a window into the grief that comes with it, because you're not just hurting yourself. You're hurting your family and your friends. You're hurting people not even in that equation. You don't even think about the people you're going to affect, but it ends up affecting them.

CHAPTER FIVE
The Beginning of FATE ~ Reggie Speaks

I spend a lot of my time these days telling Brandon's story to schools, to community groups, lawyer groups—just about anyone who will listen. It's not easy for me. One day I was feeling so bad that I couldn't suck it up and tell my story to this school. I didn't think I could make it. Then I thought *you know what, I'm not doing this by myself; I'll just act like Brandon's with me.* I just embraced that idea, and I decided when I go to schools, I will tell them, "This is what I do to hang around with my son." I believe there's merit in that. I couldn't do this alone, but maybe he and I can together. So that's what we're trying to do.

Addiction is a huge problem. I've lived in Oklahoma my whole life. I love Oklahoma people. I think it's the greatest state in the union; I wouldn't live anywhere else. However, with that said, I didn't know we had this incredible battle going on here. I think I know the reason why. I worked my way through college and law school, and I was too busy to realize what was going on. Then, after graduation, I had a busy law practice to work in. I think we tend to put our heads down. We're trying to make a living for our families and we don't look up and see what's going on around us in the area of substance abuse. That's what I was doing.

I was making a living for my family, taking care of my friends, my kids; I wasn't trying to find out what was going on in the rest of the world. Well, since my son died of this, I've researched it every day, every single day. Every night before I go to bed, I'm doing an internet search looking for literature. I drive all my friends crazy because I send them all these articles.

Now, if you don't believe me, let me just give you some data. AIDS. AIDS killed, according to the research I did, a little over 17, 000 people in the world last year. Now, that's a pandemic. It's bad. We don't have statistics that tell how many people die of substance abuse each year. Not that I can find. So I broke it down. Pick one topic: alcohol. 75,000 died in the United States alone because of alcohol. Now, tell me we don't have a pandemic. It's worse than AIDS.

The number of people we have dying is huge. But we don't have a data base that puts them all together. That's a huge problem. I grew up in the '60's during the Vietnam War, and I used to watch the news every night with my parents. We would see the "body count" in Vietnam. The bodies kept adding up, and I believe that was one of the main things that turned the tide of public opinion against the war in Vietnam. Well, we have the same thing going on here. We have dead bodies piling up in this state and in this country. It's just the news media isn't doing what it did with the Vietnam War. It's not piling the bodies up every night. Why is it not doing that? I'm not sure, but if you lose a family member like I did, you're going to start paying attention to this.

I read the paper every morning, and I watch the news every morning. How many stories do we see? Every day there are stories about people being killed in car crashes, little children being abused and neglected, acts of domestic violence. I've reached the point where I can pretty much tell whether alcohol or drugs were involved, even if the news story doesn't mention it. Most of these bad events we hear about are, at their root, caused or contributed to by substance abuse.

My son's death certificate said he died of "blunt force trauma to the back of his head"; it doesn't say substance abuse, but that's what really killed Brandon. There's no box you can check on the autopsy report, so he doesn't go into a box. Not that kind. We should have something like that, but we don't.

How many kids are dying of this? We don't know. But we do know this, the average age when kids start drinking and doing drugs in this state and this country today is twelve. Twelve, can you believe that? Something's changed. It wasn't that way when I was a kid.

We know that kids are dropping like flies. Just pick up the newspaper, and you'll see it every day. In this past year, there were twelve middle school girls that took prescription drugs at one school. They all dropped like flies. None of them died, but they were all taken to the hospital. They were taking pills one of the girls stole from her parent. After that, some college kids near Ada, Oklahoma ordered a drug off the internet to experiment with. They didn't even know what it was. Most or all of them were apparently pretty good kids. Some of them were about to graduate from college. Two of them dropped dead. The rest got very ill, and one of them is now in jail on murder charges.

There is an epidemic in our state. I love Oklahoma. I love Oklahoma and Oklahoma State football. Our teams are usually vying to be number 1 in the national polls, right? Well, Oklahoma is number 1 in prescription drug abuse. Can you explain that to me? Why would Oklahoma be number 1 ahead of California or Texas? That's insane. But we are. We are number 1 in prescription drug abuse in this country.

No other state in this country does more meth than we do. Can you explain that to me?

It's insane. Why doesn't everybody know about this problem? That's one of the goals we have with FATE We've got to make everybody aware. I'm telling you, if any parents are out there reading this, if you don't think your kids are going to experiment with this, then you've got your head in the sand. No one is immune.

I did not think there was a chance in hell my boy was going to do it, and I was wrong. They're all going to be hit by the same thing my son got hit with, which is peer pressure. They're all going to hear from that guy, you know, the buddy, the pal who comes to them and says, "Take one of these; they're not addictive."

When I was in Africa recently, we took a device called a water straw. It's incredibly engineered with a filtering system that allows you to drink out of a polluted stream or pond. The bad water passes through this water straw filter, and you can drink the water and not get sick. I was trying to talk some of the American young people we took with us to drink through it, but they wouldn't. You can stick it in the worst water in the country and drink it, and the engineers, these scientists, guarantee it's going to come out clean.

But none of these kids wanted to drink out of it. They didn't believe the scientists. Yet if their buddy comes over and says "Take one of these pills; it won't hurt you" they'd probably do it. How do you explain that?

The only way I can explain it is children, young people, will listen to their friends above all else. Peer pressure is incredibly powerful. Young people can go virtually anywhere and get alcohol. They can get tobacco products, they can order drugs off the internet, drugs we never even heard of. It's getting worse, and it's going to continue to get worse until we do something about it.

If you're a parent and you're sitting there saying, "My kid comes from a great family, was raised the right way...going to church. No way is he or she going to do these things." You're wrong. They can, and they will. Some of the best and brightest of our kids in this state are doing it. The poorest and least well off kids in the state are doing it, too. It cuts across class, race, neighborhoods, religions (or no religion). It is no respecter of persons.

No, they are not all going to get killed by it. Some will die, but some will live and have their lives ruined by it. Still others will use alcohol, marijuana or some other drugs and will go on to live "normal lives". Why does substance abuse treat people differently? Well, this is where it gets complicated. Not everybody has a genetic predisposition to get addicted. The Commissioner of the Oklahoma Department of Mental Health and Substance Abuse Services, Terri White, tells me that studies show that about 10 percent of the population has this propensity to get hooked.

Why do we use that word "hooked"? It's a pretty good analogy. Fish don't jump on your hook by accident; we trick them into getting on there. Once they get on the hook, they can't get off, right? That's how these drugs are. My boy took the bait. Just like a fish and he didn't know he couldn't get off. He was part of that percentage of the population that gets hooked.

We try to teach our kids when they're young "Don't touch the hot stove!" Well, 100 percent of the people who touch the hot stove get burned. That's how kids learn. But with drugs and alcohol, these kids, my kids, your kids, they're seeing some of their friends touch the hot stove, and they're not getting burned. So they conclude it's safe. That's the insidious nature of this thing. Not everybody gets burned. But many do. The thing is, you don't know whether you're one of the ones who is going to get burned. I recently spoke at a "sober high school" where young people who are addicted can finish their high school degree in a supportive, recovery based environment. I asked the students what could have been done to keep them from experimenting with drugs and one of the kids told me, "I don't think there's anything you could have done. I think every kid has to touch his own hot stove." I hope that's not true.

You might ask, "Well, Reggie, I'm sorry you lost your kid, but what are we supposed to do?" I don't have all the answers. I never did, and I don't today. But what do you do when you have an epidemic? You begin by learning all you can and then taking action. You don't have to have all the answers before you take action, do you? I mean when we first found out about AIDS, we didn't have all the answers. We don't have a cure today. The first step was becoming aware. You have to be aware that there's something out there killing our kids.

Then, you've got to spread that word. You've got to make the truth known. Addiction is not just bad people doing bad things. You can't just lock them all up in prison and throw away the key. We cannot financially afford to lock everybody that takes drugs up in a prison. It costs around twenty three thousand dollars a year to lock somebody up. Do they come out of there better? No. they come out of there worse.

We've got to do something differently, and I think the first step is awareness. I'm not proud that I had to bury my son and his girlfriend before I became aware. I'm not proud of that. I'm deeply ashamed about it. But I'm not going to sit here and cry about a past I cannot change. I'm not going to fold up my tent and just walk away. I'm going to try to get people to be aware of the truth. Then, they can make their own judgment and, hopefully, take action.

Hopefully we can stimulate enough knowledge that people will get interested. Maybe we'll find a way out of this problem. But we've got to turn this around. We've got to change the culture. It's the worst problem facing our state and our nation. My boy is just one of many who are dying from this pandemic.

Jim Priest Speaks

In November 2010, I had just lost a statewide election for Oklahoma Attorney General. In the aftermath of that loss, I planned to return to practicing law and began re-entering the world of representing clients and appearing in court. Then one morning my law partner Reg called me.

"Hey, what are you going to do now that you lost the election?"

"Thanks for the reminder, Reg. I guess I'm going to go back to practicing law."

"I've got a better idea. Why don't you come and run the nonprofit I've formed, FATE It will be more fun than being Attorney General and nobody will shoot at you."

It sounded like an intriguing idea—especially the part about not being shot at. But it would be a big step to leave my career of 30 plus years and take on an embryonic nonprofit organization. After much prayer and thought, I agreed to do it.

My learning curve was steep. I had no background in substance abuse other than random things I had learned through practicing law for thirty plus years. But one of the most memorable things that stuck with me from my statewide campaign for Attorney General was how many people talked to me about substance abuse.

On my very first day on the campaign trail, I talked with a notable local person who told me after my speech, "The first thing you need to do after you win is legalize marijuana!" I told the person that was not likely. First of all, the Attorney General can't just "legalize" things. But more importantly, I do not believe marijuana should be legalized. While it's true that we have far too many people in jails for small drug offenses, we have to recognize that marijuana is a harmful substance, and it shouldn't be legalized simply because the laws are hard to enforce.

In every county I traveled to during the campaign, I would talk to judges, district attorneys and law enforcement officers. I asked them, "If I'm fortunate enough to be elected, what could I do to help you?" Almost without exception they said "Do something about alcohol and drugs. It drives 80% of what we do in the criminal justice system." I've since found out they are right.

Substance abuse invades every nook and cranny of our lives and, as Reggie says, it is no respecter of persons. I know this because two of our very good friends were dramatically affected by substance abuse. Here's their story:

Wes & Lori Video

A conversation with Wes and Dr. Lori Hansen

Lori: I'm Lori Hanson Lane, and I do facial plastic surgery. My husband Wes is a lawyer.

Wes: I've been a practicing attorney for many years and served as Oklahoma County District Attorney for five years.

Lori: About ten years ago, I developed some compressed disks in my back which cause me tremendous pain, so I went to a neurosurgeon, and he prescribed some pain pills for me. I took it as prescribed, but the thing I didn't realize was that I became addicted. I thought that if you were addicted you craved something and you were manic. What was happening to me was at the end of the day, I was so fatigued I could barely lift a finger. The only thing that gave me energy to finish my day was to take a pain pill.

As all of that was evolving, my staff started paying attention to the number of samples that were missing from our office and the number of prescriptions that I was writing. So they sat down and confronted me, and I thought I was the most miserable slime-bag that ever walked the earth.

Wes: It was totally shocking to me. Where had the clues been? I had no idea that she had actually been abusing narcotics.

Lori: Wes, I felt, had basically left me psychologically because he was struggling; he didn't know what to do. I have never felt so alone in my life. I stopped taking those pain pills on June fourth of 2000 and haven't picked it up again. I went to treatment and was able to successfully treat my addiction.

Wes: And that literally seemed to be the end of it.

Lori: I had this routine reapplication for my medical license with the Oklahoma State Medical Licensure Board. One of the questions the form asked was, "Have you ever been to treatment?" And shoot, yeah, I had, so I checked the yes. I really didn't know what was getting ready to happen. It was Wes that was called by the Attorney General. He said "Listen, we're going after your wife."

Wes: It was like the ultimate irony. I'm the District Attorney, charged with prosecuting drug cases, and now someone's investigating my wife. And that really became quite a media sensation. It was in everything from the USA Today to the Los Angeles Times. I think for the first time I actually understood what these families were going through.

Lori: There are a huge number of people that are addicted to drugs and alcohol. Those of you who are not addicted to anything need to understand addiction is an illness; it is not a character defect. Going through this process it would have been great if I had had a human – any human – say, "I understand what you're going through. I love you; you are not a slime bag."

I'm Wes Lane. I'm Doctor Lori Hansen. What's YOUR fate?

Jim Priest Speaks

I've concluded that one of the most important things we can do to fight addiction is to fight the misconceptions and the stigma that accompany addictions. The fact that Lori and Wes are willing to speak out should be a great encouragement to others who might think they cannot talk about their addiction. Lori recently appeared before the Oklahoma Medical Licensure Board and was taken off the indefinite probation that had been imposed on her. Here's the article from the Oklahoman newspaper.

**Oklahoma medical panel takes Dr. Lori Hansen
off indefinite probation**

Full medical privileges restored to Dr. Lori Hansen

BY JACLYN COSGROVE | Published: July 13, 2012

A state medical panel took Dr. Lori Hansen off indefinite probation Thursday, restoring full medical privileges to an award-winning plastic surgeon. Hansen, the wife of a former prosecutor, has waged a public battle against her addiction to narcotics.

The action Thursday by the Oklahoma Board of Medical Licensure and Supervision means Hansen can again write prescriptions for controlled substances and will not be subject to restrictions some insurance companies and medical organizations have regarding doctors on probation.

Lyle Kelsey, the Oklahoma Medical Board executive director, said Hansen has been sober for about five years. The board has found through its research of doctors with substance abuse issues that when someone hits the five-year sobriety mark, he or she can usually lead successful careers, he said.

Over the past 10 years, Hansen, 59, has been before the board several times for issues related to substance abuse.

Last year, she told The Oklahoman about her struggle with addiction.

"If the Lord gave me this path to walk, He did so for a reason. I want to honor Him by giving Him glory for getting me through it," she said.

She began taking hydrocodone in 1997 for back pain after car accidents and eventually got to the point where she would take the drug from the sample cabinet at her office or write her own prescriptions. Her staff confronted her about her drug problem in 2000.

A former Miss Oklahoma USA, Hansen has appeared on numerous national television talk shows and in 2011 won a national award for best surgical facial rejuvenation.

On Wednesday, Gov. Mary Fallin appointed Hansen's husband, Wes Lane, former Oklahoma County district attorney, as chairman of the Oklahoma Commission for Human Services.

We're terrifically proud of Lori and Wes, their integrity, and their commitment to each other and to dealing with this issue in an honest and forthright way.

Another one of our friends, Kelly Dyer Fry also stepped out and spoke about her struggle with the addiction of her son. In fact, Kelly, who is the editor of the Oklahoman, spoke out about it in a headliner article which appeared on the front page of Oklahoma's largest newspaper on Mother's Day 2011.   People like Lori and Wes and Kelly and Reggie are providing great examples of how to defeat the stigma that attaches to addiction. We have to overcome the stigma in order to deal with addiction. In the next chapter, you'll read Kelly's story in her own words.

Reprinted with permission from The Oklahoman.

CHAPTER SIX
A Thousand Hail Mary's

Sometimes, I like to picture an event in the way I imagine God sees it. My friend and I take our places on the crowded dance floor. How can you pass up a chance to crash a plate on the floor? I'm in Kansas City at a Greek restaurant. Dancing. Laughing.

My son is in Florida. He's high again. Driving deep into a high-crime area holding the belief he can rip off a drug dealer. He tries to pass a wad of cash, six one dollar bills, to the dealer and take the drugs simultaneously. The seasoned dealer knows the gig. A gun is pulled, the car speeds off, shots are fired. Four bullets hit the car, one travels through the taillight, the back seat, the front seat and into my son's back.

I wonder what God saw? I wonder if the shots coincided with my crashing plate? My heels click against the tile as I walk down the hall toward my son's bedroom. I'm still in my suit from work. Wanted to get in a half day at least. I work for a media company as a vice president. I sit in executive meetings and look to my right and my left. Does anyone else in here have a kid shooting heroin? Doubtful. I share my story sometimes. Not often.

I've walked down this hall too many times. So much trepidation. I hear my heart in my head. Will he be dead this time? Today I see his chest rise and fall. There is hope. "Get up! Get up right now!" I'm screaming at my 22-year-old son to get out of bed. He's stretched across the bed, beer cans strewed on the floor. The carpet is sticky. He has an itchy wool blanket covering the window. I flip on the light. His color is gray, dark circles under his eyes. He's so very thin, gaunt really. He hasn't showered in days. His jeans are frayed on the ends and carry the deep wrinkles of unwashed clothes. The tattoo across his chest reads: "I Need More." So do I. I need more for him. I need more for our family. I need more peace, and I need him to live.

A part of me has accepted the fact he may not. A part of me actually acknowledges death may bring him peace. Who thinks that? What kind of mother have I become?

"We are going. You can go get in the car, or you can just go." My hands are on my hips, two feet planted.

I'm remembering him now in his navy slacks, white shirt and red plaid tie. His dress uniform for Catholic School. He's 12 years old and standing at the front of the church on Christmas Eve, swaying. He always sways when he sings. "Midnight silence calm as the sky," he sings his solo in front of packed pews.

Hail Mary, Full of Grace

I start praying in my head, almost chanting. "Please, please get up. You said you would go." I don't cry anymore. I'm numb, robotic. Crying lost impact on my son years ago. I am stoic. I'm remembering a time when I sank in tears to the kitchen floor as he smashed a plate across the tile. It splintered. "Oh, that's great, Mom," he shouts. "Let's go for the f-----g drama... Whatever." He snarls as he bolts out the front door. Gone. Gone into the night. Who knows where.

Is he meeting up with people who have gangster names like Snake and Storm? I can't even believe names like that are in my vocabulary. How did it happen? How did it get so ridiculous? How did we catapult from beer to heroin?

"I'm not going. I changed my mind," he says. Get out of my room you f-----g b---h" How? Why?

Eric on a bad day
Photo by Stephanie A. Smith

I stand firm. I'm so hardened by this language. It no longer cuts to my heart. This is not really my son talking. Not my little boy. This is a junkie. A heroin junkie.

"I'm not kidding. This time I'm serious. You can go to Florida, or you can just go. It's your choice, but you can't stay here."

I think about his first run-in with alcohol. His cousin is getting married, and it's fun for his cousins to let the eighth grader have a sip here and there. He plays the game around the room, and before you know it, he is in the bathroom throwing up. Grandma hands him a cold rag. She laughs, "I bet he won't drink wine anymore." Everyone has those stories. Don't they? Kid tries drinking, throws up, you hope they learn from mistakes. I know intimately now that some kids move past that stage. For some, a hole opens up and swallows them ... and you go, too. Everyone starts sliding. Sliding into the dark hole.

Sam, Kelly and Eric at the wedding where Eric first drank alcohol

He's calling my bluff. I have to be resolute.

Hail Mary, full of grace. The Lord is with me. Blessed art thou among women and blessed is the fruit of thy womb, Jesus. Holy Mary Mother of God, pray for us sinners now and at the hour of our death. Hail Mary...

"I'm calling Ed and Mandy and getting my job back," he barks. They won't take him back; I know this. They care enough about him to let him fall. After years of struggling, I do, too. I still can't bring myself to let him roam the streets of Oklahoma City. I'm not as strong as some of the parents who cut their children off in an effort to save their lives. I know Eric would never stand for it. He most likely would end up on his brother's couch. It's too much to ask of my youngest son, Sam. Junkies have vast networks of enablers. It would be months of imposing on others before he landed in the streets. I believe he doesn't have time on his side anymore. I believe he will die soon.

I look him in the eye and say slowly, enunciating each word like I did when he was young.

"We. Are. Going. You will not talk me out of it. Just get in the car. Now."

"OK, but I'm not shower-ing."

Just another assault. Just a silly gesture to show he's still in control.

Top: Eric's first communion.

Bottom: Brothers, Eric 5 and Sam 2

"Fine," I shrug. I have already packed his clothes, and the car is loaded. He walks to the car without a shirt on. A blanket is wrapped around his shoulders, dragging behind his bare, dirty feet. I'm driving his used Honda Accord. This is one of many cars I have bought my son. He once gave one away to a dealer he owed money. Of course, that makes no sense. And why would I buy him another one? When you are living in the dark world of drugs, everyone's will and logic is askew.

I want to do the right thing as the parent of an addict. But there's something that prevents me from having the strength. I've made plenty of bad decisions and plenty of good ones. It's a roll of the dice every single day. An addict will test you over and over and over again. He will wear you down and zap you of all your energy. There are some days I only put one foot in front of the other. A good friend once told me angels only come to your aid when you invite them. "Angels, Angels, Angels," I repeat in almost a "Beetlejuice" chant. I picture my angels like Secret Service men. They walk beside me, steadying me. They talk into their wrists and say things like, "I got this one." I let go. Let go and let God. I've heard this statement many times as I sat in a folding chair behind the sign shop at an Al-Anon meeting. I went faithfully for many years. I learned a lot from those people. Inner strength. They are impressive. I keep meaning to go back to another meeting. Tired. I just get tired of being the mother of an addict.

Finally, we are in the car. "I need cigarettes," he shouts. "I can't do this. I'm going to be dope sick." We are 50 hours away from West Palm Beach. We are going to the Sunset House. I know of this place due to the kindness of strangers. I posted to an Internet message board. Parents Helping Parents in Edmond has a dedicated group of bruised parents who stand shoulder to shoulder and fight valiantly to save their children or yours. I wrote that I was out of money and out of ideas. Eric's addiction bill soared well beyond $100,000. I got an email then a phone call from the founder of the group. I've spoken to this kind man before. Six years ago when my son was a senior in high school, he spoke frankly to me on the phone when I told him I didn't think I could force my son into treatment, because he was 17 years old. That's too old. Right? According to the law? "What do you think will happen to you?" he said firmly. "Do you think someone's going to come arrest you? Put that young man in the car and get him there." So I did just that. That day we had two cars. My older brother and I rode in one. Eric, his brother Sam and a friend were in the other. More antics. More bad negotiation with a young addict. Seventeen years old.

As we made our way to Hazelstreet in Texarkana, the trip started unraveling. It ended with a foot chase in a small town. I called 911, and the local boys showed up with guns in hand. "He's just a scared kid," I screamed. "Put that gun back in your holster. Now." Crazy mothers scare people. They did as asked. He eventually stayed 90 days at Hazelstreet. That's what we agreed upon before he went. I learn later how silly it is to negotiate a length of stay with an addict. Nonetheless, he learned about addiction. It was his first foray into education of the disease. The staff was tremendous, and he was safe for at least 90 days. His brother and I enjoyed the peace and quiet.

Eric and Sam visit outside Hazelstreet in Texarkana

This time the Parents Helping Parents gentleman came to my rescue again. He asked if he could give my phone number to another mom who knew of some programs that might be of interest. A couple days later, I get a call from a soft-spoken mom. She asked me to meet her for lunch that day. Moms know not to put things off when dealing with addicts. Any second could be their last. She mentions I will recognize her because she is bald. "I've been undergoing chemo," she says. I'm humbled. God has sent me another angel. This one has a scarf around her head and she has reached out mother to mother. Amazing. Grace. She tells me how her son went to Sunset House in West Palm Beach and how he's now in college studying to be a chemical dependency counselor. I have always secretly held the dream that Eric would someday use his speaking talents to reach others. I always try to make sense of all this. If something good could just come of all this. Anything. My son was a state finalist debater in high school. He has great speaking abilities and wins friends with ease.

I know in my heart that he and I need space between us. We are tangled up. One of us breathes in, the other out. We pull together then push apart. His maturity stopped when he was about 16. Drugs took over then. I watched as his brother, three years his younger passed him emotionally. I fought hard to stop his descent into addiction. I held on tightly. Too tightly.

We pass Tinker Air Force Base on I-40 East. I want to point out the window like I did when he was a small child and say, "Look at the planes." But I sit in silence, white knuckles on the steering wheel.

Hail Mary, Full of grace

He starts to shiver. I'm a little worried he might jump from the moving car, but I take solace in the fact he buckled his seat belt. There's a part of him that wants to survive. "You're going to have to stop," he says as his teeth start to chatter. We've only been on the road for 20 minutes. Florida is a long way off. Must drive. Must keep going. I don't know if I'm running away from something or running toward something. Confusion.

The Lord is with me, blessed art thou among women

I pull off the interstate to a gas station. He pulls on a shirt. No shoes. "I need some money." This sets off an emotion. A struggle. Every time I hand him money, I get a pit in my stomach. This time seems harmless enough. He comes out of the gas station with a paper sack. In it is a large beer, the kind with tomato juice already mixed in. "I have to drink this. It's going to be really hard to detox on the way to Florida. We can't make it." We will make it. Angels, angels, angels.

Another one of those reality moments smacks me in the face. I'm driving with my son down the interstate as he sips beer. I make him pour it in a large Sonic cup. How? Why? This is ridiculous. I tell myself to keep going.

Top Left: Eric, age 15 months. Top Right: Christmas ages 5 (Eric) and 2 (Sam). Bottom Left: Eric, freshman year at Edmond Memorial High School. Bottom Right: Sam, Kelly and Eric skiing in Red River

I'm remembering when Eric was about 2 years old. He's outside playing in the snow. He's wearing a red coat that is so full it makes his arms stick out. He's plowing slowly through a drift. It's almost waist high for him. I hear him repeating, "Keeeeep going. Keeeeep going."

That's what I will do today. Keeeep going.

And Blessed Is The Fruit Of Thy Womb, Jesus

We are trying to reach Memphis by evening. We left OKC just before noon. Eric is still fidgeting. He can't sit still. He's sweating then freezing. Agitated. He wants more beer though we have stopped several times for him to fill up his Route 44 Sonic cup. We also stop frequently for him to go to the bathroom. He tries watching the DVD player. I have a sack full of movies. The whole second season of one of his favorite TV shows, *House*. I can't really hear the movie, so

I have a book on tape, *The Book Thief.* It's a good book, but my mind wanders. I constantly have to back up and find my place. I give up. I switch to Pandora. The music seems to add a bizarre soundtrack to our long drive. My firstborn son is smoking cigarettes. Sipping on a beer. I'm driving. Searching. Is there anyone who will help my son? Will someone look beyond the shaggy haired young man and see the desperation in his eyes. I check to see if his seat belt is still on. Yes. Hope.

We pull into Memphis. It's dusk. We need to find a pharmacy. Maybe Benadryl can ease his crawly skin. "It feels like it's on fire. Make it stop." He stammers as his teeth click. I decide to pull off the Interstate and find a store. Wrong turn. The exit I have taken is deep into a very rough part of Memphis. There are droves of men standing next to barrels with fire shooting from the top. It looks like a movie scene. They are openly smoking pipes. Meth? Crack? I don't know. It's Halloween and mothers dressed in short skirts are teetering on high heels as they walk their children down the sidewalks. There's Spiderman. A princess. It's a stark contrast. Hookers, dealers, batman, mamas, ghosts, junkies, strollers. Broken humanity. What

chance do these mothers have to keep their children off drugs. I lived in Edmond and spent every penny I had to send my children to Catholic school. I was a homeroom mom and volunteered in the lunchroom. I vowed that my children would not miss out on my involvement at their school. I would never lean on the fact I was a working, single mom.

Top: Eric, home for Easter
Bottom: Mom and son pose
for a photo during a visit home

"Mom, pull over. It's so easy. I can score. Pull over, Stop. Hurry." Eric is rambling. Speaking nonsense, gibberish. His voice has taken on the quality of someone I don't recognize: "Come on, pull over, Baby. Whatchou doin?" Who is he? I speed forward trying to make my way to a safer part of town. It seems like I drive for miles before I find my way back on the Interstate. His voice is back to normal. He shakes his head. For the first time in eight hours he speaks to me in a civil tone. "Oh. My. Gosh. Mom, did you hear me back there? It's like I really thought you would pull over. How crazy is that?"

Holy Mary Mother Of God, Pray For Us Sinners Now And At The Hour Of Our Death

I want to press on, but my left leg is aching. My neck is in knots and that one spot on my left shoulder blade is burning. Stress brings on the hot poker. Eric is in no condition to help drive. He's nauseous now, gagging periodically. He stares out the side window. He's always done this in a car. I remember looking back at him in his car seat. He would gaze out the side window the whole trip. It's a metaphor for how he does life. He rarely looks forward. If you look forward, you might see danger, obstacles, consequences.

An hour or so beyond Memphis we stop. It's a motel. We are on the second-floor balcony. I want to call my husband, Eric's step-father. I want to connect with reality. But I can't call in front of Eric. I can't carry on a conversation with him listening. I want to tell my husband that I am hurting. I want to hear his voice, his support. Eric steps out on the balcony to smoke a cigarette. I worry that he may somehow steal away into the night. I play scenarios through my head. I play " what if." I make a few phone calls, but I can't really express what I am feeling. I'm in a fog. When your child is sick, it can be very lonely. Everyone offers support but it's like childbirth — it comes down to you and your child. Through the years, other parents stopped asking about Eric. They thought they were being kind, not wanting to embarrass me. But I wanted to scream. Please don't give up on my child. He's a fighter. He has to pull through. I told Eric many years ago I would never give up. "I'm fighting if you're fighting. Any given day," I would say. "Any given day you can turn it all around." I don't know how many times I have asked God to let my child live long enough to get help. I'm a glass half-full person. Every trip to rehab would be his last. I'm remembering his trip to a 90-day stint at Narconon. We had a particularly rough event that led to that stay. As young boys, Eric and his brother had a saying: "I'm going to hit you in the face." It was an empty threat. Neither of them had ever struck his own brother in the face. Until that night. Eric was frantic, high. He said he owed money to a dealer and feared retaliation. Another mistake on my part. What to do? I go to the ATM at 7-11 and withdraw $400. I live in a crazy world of fear and desperation. I don't belong here. How? Why? When I return, Eric wants to leave. I grab his keys, and he pulls back. His brother joins in and the three of us are in a wrestling match. Then it happens. Eric hits his brother in the face. Unspeakable. Unforgivable. We all know we have crossed into new territory. We stop. We look at each other. Eric grabs the keys and runs out the door. His brother yells. "Why did you let him go, Mom? Why?" I can't answer. I am broken, frozen. His brother has sacrificed too much. He's been my rock. Very stable at too young of an age. I will not allow violence to break this family even further.

When Eric returns he knows the world looks differently now. He struck his brother in the face. He agrees to go to treatment. I get on the phone, start calling places. Anyplace. He needs help. His brother and I do, too. He leaves for Narconon the next day. Neither of us knows much about it, but it's an immediate relief. We need that. I put $10,000 on a credit card. He stays for 90 days. Strange experience, but once again — a much-needed break from his drug use.

Eric, Kelly and Sam before the Oklahoma Outreach
Foundation dinner in October

I don't know if this trip will be any different, but I have to try. I've run out of options. Maybe I'm finally ready to "Let go and let God," as they say in Al-Anon. Telling a mother to let go of her child is hard to comprehend, believe me. But I know he won't live if he doesn't put distance between him and the dealers. He told me how easy it was to get heroin. How he'd see mothers driving minivans with kids in car seats lined up to pick up their fix. Or men in nice cars wearing business suits. "You never really know, Mom," he said. "It's more people than you would ever think."

It's late now. The room is dark except for the glow of the television. Eric showered and is leaning against two pillows clicking through channels on the TV. He tells me his skin hurts. "Mom, remember when we used to watch ER," he says. "Yeah," I say. Silence. We both know he was referring to better days. We don't have to talk to have understanding. I breathe in, he breathes out.

I wake up early. We slept with the TV on. I shower and go to the lobby for breakfast. I look around the small room. An older couple is sharing conversation over their Styrofoam bowls of cereal. I wonder what life has dealt them. Did they have children? Grandchildren? Has addiction been a part of their family story? I've heard addiction affects 50 percent of our population. If you are not an addict, you have still been affected by one. I balance my bagel and coffee, stick a banana under my arm. I grab a muffin, too. Maybe Eric will eat something. I head for the elevator, and the woman I had seen in the lobby is getting on the

elevator at the same time. She has gray hair; I think she's a snowbird headed south. I want to drop everything and fall into her arms. In my head I am saying "Please, help me. Pray for me and my son." The bell dings, we both get off. She smiles tenderly. Maybe she heard me, I think.

I get back to the room and Eric is still in bed. "Please get up. We have to get going." He snarls, but rolls out of bed and begins to complain. "Oh my God," he says. "It's not any better. When will it get better?" I realize I will face another day of driving. No help is coming. Keep going.

Eric in West Palm Beach

Eric is not much better today, but seems to be resigned that we are not turning back. He doesn't sleep much, but when he does, I try to be totally quiet. Just like when he was a toddler taking a morning nap. That's when I got the beds made, laundry going as quietly as possible. If I was lucky, I could sit down and read the paper; but only if I was really quiet. Now his sleep brings some semblance of peace within our car. By 11 a.m. he's drinking beer again. Less than yesterday, so maybe that's an improvement. I have no idea what the open container laws are in Tennessee. When you are struggling with heroin withdrawal, open container laws seem trivial. Logic gets skewed when you are sliding deeper and deeper into the hole.

Just three months earlier, I was driving Eric to a rehab center in Cushing. He spent 30 days there, just long enough to fully detox and clear his head. His heart was filled with hope and promise, but that's the way it works for addicts. They don't intend to relapse. They don't do it to hurt you. Sometimes, I see HOPE in all caps. Sometimes, I can barely see it. I held lots of hope after his stay in Cushing, but it started to flicker just days after he was home. He was staying in an Oxford House with other recovering addicts and alcoholics. It's a haven with its own democratic rules and accountability. Good system, he just was not ready. As I've heard so many times, some folks hit bottom and keep digging.

We are through Chattanooga now and heading on to Atlanta. I see a truck ahead of us and notice a wobbly tire and faint black smoke. I slow down and say, "Watch that tire; it's about to come off." It does, and he looks at me with wonder. "How did you know that?" I tell him I was paying attention, looking ahead, watching. He gives me a look. He knows I'm trying to make it a life lesson about learning to anticipate what lies ahead. He lives his life looking in the rearview mirror, seldom wondering what his actions may bring.

It is a tremendous blessing that my son has never been in serious trouble with the law. His only brush with the police was when his car tag was written down by a convenience store clerk. It involved a foolish prank of yelling "yeehaw" and running out the store with a 12-pack of beer. He went to the police station to turn himself in. They actually laughed at him for doing so. He got a slap on the wrist and no permanent record of the incident. But he's always been lucky. And in many cases lucky to be alive. He once fell about 25 feet through a tree he was climbing. The limbs broke his fall all the way down to the sidewalk. He's been hit by two different teen drivers: once, when he was 4 riding his three wheeler in the cul-de-sac and another time when a teenage girl thought she had cleared his front bike tire, but instead threw him into the curb. For once he was wearing his helmet.

When he was 20, night terrors sent him soaring through a second-story window. He landed headfirst in a row of shrubs. His roommate called me to come to the hospital. The nurse stopped me outside his room and asked if blood made me queasy. I said no, but was not really prepared for what I saw. His chest and stomach were covered in blood-soaked gauze. His leg looked like it had been cut open with a garden hoe. I could see muscle and bone. His wrist was broken. When he hit the ground, he jumped to his feet and ran up the street. He left a trail of blood I would later clean with peroxide. Take two steps, stop and pour peroxide on the deep red stain. Watch the bubble wash away the terror. The wrist surgery offered a new high for my son.

He loved hydrocodone. He pulled his cast off one day and called me screaming that he had to go see the doctor. His doctor was wise and after poking around his hand discovered that he did not have consistent reaction to pain. He looked me in the eye and said he would not give my son more pain medication. "I lost a bright, young intern once to pain killers. I won't contribute to this." We left with a new cast and very few pain relievers. But the trigger had been pulled. He liked the new high and would start a new chase. Addicts love new highs.

Eric feeding the wildlife at Jupiter Pier

He has slowed his drinking and seems to be sleeping more now. I drive and I drive and I drive. It is sheer will that keeps me going. As a child, one of my favorite toys was a blow up clown with sand in the bottom. I loved it when he always popped back up. I'm the one now that has to add sand to my shoes. I have to keep standing back up to fight another day. Exhaustion. Hot poker in my left shoulder blade. The second day of driving passes in a blur. We stop just north of the Florida border. I want to press on, but I am out of strength.

Neither of us is sleeping well, so we decide to get up about 5 a.m. and continue our drive. We stop for breakfast at a waffle house that seems like it's in the middle of nowhere. It is empty except for a couple of guys loitering outside the front door. We order. Once we get our food, the cook wanders outside to talk to the men smoking cigarettes by the front door. We look at each other nervously, something doesn't feel right. We eat quickly. Our bill comes to the table. It is twice the amount it should be. "Mom, just pay it. We need to leave right now." He has an innate sense for trouble. That's probably what has kept him alive in some dangerous situations. I leave $40 cash on the table and hurry to the car. "Don't make eye contact, Mom." Back in the car, a sigh of relief. I'm encouraged by his protective attitude. My son loves me deeply. He does not mean to hurt me. Addicts are not punishers. They are very sick people in need of help. I know this in my head, but my heart still carries sadness. Did I fail as a mom? Did I fail to protect him?

Once we enter Florida, we begin to see signs to Orlando. He's only had a couple beers today. As we get closer to Orlando, we begin to see the Disney signs. Stops for gas bring back memories of taking the kids to Disney World. I see families with matching colored shirts headed for the theme parks. Some have names on the back like Daddy, Mommy or Grandma. I hear kids asking for stuffed Disney characters. I once was one of those parents. Taking my sons, 7 and 10, along with my niece to Disney World. It seems like yesterday. I wonder what's in store for these families. Today I feel miles away from the magic of Disney.

Finally, West Palm Beach. Our plan is to stay one night in a hotel then check in the next day to Sunset House. We have talked to them by phone many times. They are expecting us the next day. We check into a beachside hotel with hopes of getting a good night's rest. He is still sick, but it now seems to come in waves. He's nervous about checking in without being fully detoxed. We go for a walk on the beach. The tension is palpable. He knows I am leaving the next day without him. My flight is booked for the afternoon. Exhausted, I go to bed early. In the morning, I go down to the beach for a walk. I sit, drink coffee. The ocean feels like a healing place. I pray. I plead. I pray for wisdom, patience and perseverance. I must leave my son here. I must go.

Hail Mary, Full Of Grace...

People at the Sunset House are very supportive. I check him in. I make the sign of the cross on his forehead, tell him I love him and get in the cab to drive away. The Lord is with thee, blessed art thou among women and blessed is the fruit of thy womb, Jesus. Holy Mary mother of God, pray for us sinners now and at the hour of our death, Amen.

Of course, that's not the end. But it does prove to be a beginning. Within weeks he is asked to leave the Sunset House. He has not stopped using. New drug connections were made within days of moving to his new city. I tell him he cannot come home. He moves to another halfway house which proves to be disastrous.

My husband and I are in Kansas City with friends. We just got home from a Greek Restaurant with our friends. A fun night. My cellphone rings. I don't hear any words but, "Your son has been shot." Terror. By early morning, I'm on a flight to West Palm Beach. I have talked to him, and I know that he is OK. The doctors tell him the bullet will have to remain in his back. It is one inch from his spine. One inch away from a spinal cord injury. One inch away.

I pick him up in my rental car, and we drive to a nearby restaurant to talk. I have no idea what to do. I am lost. The only thing I know for sure is that he cannot stay in that place. We drive back there and a few of the men help carry his things to the car. I can tell they are not sober. This halfway house is a sham. An older gentleman leans into my car, looks me in the eye and says sincerely, "You are doing the right thing. Get him out of here."

Where do we go now? I don't have a laptop, I feel helpless, out of my element. I need to get online and explore other options. I cannot take him home. There is no future there. It would be almost a death sentence. I know the bullet in his back has brought him a new revelation. A new bottom. "Mom, they wouldn't listen to me in the hospital. I told them I was different. I had insurance. They thought I was a gang banger. They were awful." As he spoke these words, I could see in his eyes he realized what he was saying. We paused. We looked each other in the eye. No words, just understanding.

With all his belongings in the car we started driving. I didn't know where to go. We went to a Kmart where they had a bank of computers set up for public access. It's tremendously difficult to navigate a strange city. No networks. No friends. No colleagues. I take him to another emergency room to get rechecked. I want to talk to a doctor. I want to hear him say that the bullet in my son's back must stay there.

I've never felt more alone. Guns and violence have no place in my world. I'm not sure how to fit this in. How do I process this? How do I understand? I'm struggling this time to put more sand in my shoes.

When we leave Kmart, we get back in the car. I look down and see something blue sticking out from my seat. I reach down and pick up a business card from The Sunset House. I stare at it. I have no idea how it got there but I am wise enough to take it as a positive sign. I call the kind man at Sunset. "I've been worried sick," he says. "How is he. I've been calling hospitals." After a long conversation, he tells me he wants him to come back to the Sunset House. They want to try again. I feel like a miracle has been handed to us. Another chance. Hope. Our hope comes from faith. Faith that God will qualify us to persevere. Time after time we have fallen. I say we because I am his mother. It is that simple. The opposite of hope is despair. We cannot live there.

It has been just over two years since the shooting. He stayed at Sunset House for 15 months. He had a relapse when he left, but I can say *today* he is good. And I can only talk about today. But what a blessing today is.

Hail Mary, Full Of Grace, The Lord Is With Thee...

Kelly's Story Online

Reprinted with permission from The Oklahoman.

CHAPTER SEVEN
Life of An Athlete
Jim Speaks

The first order of business when we began FATE was to decide where to start. It was like being sent into the Amazon jungle to trim back the shrubs: there was so much to do. Where should we begin? Reg and I talked to people at the Oklahoma Department of Mental Health and Substance Abuse Services and one of them, Jessica Hawkins, told me about a program called "Life of An Athlete". Jessica said, "We were going to look into this substance abuse education program that focuses on high school and college athletes, but we just don't have the personnel or the money to do it. You guys know some athletes. Maybe this would be a good fit for you."

We did know some athletes. Through a series of connections, Reg had become friends with several NFL players who had travelled with him to Uganda on a Pros for Africa trip. Life of An Athlete sounded like a possibility, so I arranged to travel to Lake Placid, New York for the winter training session of Life of An Athlete.

LOA is a program started by Olympic trainer and coach John Underwood who has conducted thousands of tests on Olympic athletes and has come to some definite conclusions about the effect of alcohol and marijuana on athletic performance. John's research shows the effect is all negative. The performance of Olympic athletes is reduced by 11.4% when they drink, and the effect on college and high school athletes would be even greater. The bottom line John says is this: off the field conduct impacts on the field performance. If you want to be the best you can be as an athlete, you have to avoid alcohol and other drugs.

We've adopted and adapted John's program in Oklahoma and created a website where people can take on line training to learn about alcohol and other drugs' adverse impact on athletic performance. You can link to the training website by way of this QR:

www.okloa.org

Our organization believes young people and especially young athletes are better approached about drugs and alcohol by building on areas of their own motivation rather than telling them "Just say no". We ask the question in all our videos and presentations "What's YOUR fate?" because we want people to think about their future. The decisions we make today determine our fate in the future. But most young people think short term, not long term. They are willing to take risks and seek out short term pleasure despite the prospect for long term pain. That's part of how their brains are hardwired. So at FATE, we try to get them to think long term by appealing to areas where they are already motivated, like athletics.

Most young athletes are motivated to play their best and be their best, and once they learn about the adverse effect on performance that alcohol and other drugs can have, a light goes on. They recognize their off field conduct affects their on field performance, and by getting buzzed or drunk, they are taking steps backward in their training instead of moving forward. Here is some of the information we share with student athletes, and it has application to all of us.

"What's Your D.I.?" *(Your Drug Intelligence)*

Before reading the rest of this information about the Life of An Athlete program, test yourself by taking the following true false test:

1. Alcohol is a drug.
2. An athlete could lose up to two weeks training from getting drunk one time.
3. People who drink or use drugs are more likely to be injured.

4. Marijuana is harmless.
5. Taking prescription drugs that belong to someone else is a safe and effective way to deal with pain.
6. The ten most dangerous years of life are ages 14-24.
7. On average, teens take their first drink at age 12.
8. Alcohol and other drugs interfere with messages your brain sends to your muscles.
9. My decisions about using alcohol or other drugs should be left up to me, because I am the only one affected.
10. Children who have regular sit down meals with their family are 50% less likely to use alcohol or drugs.

Answers:

1. Alcohol is a drug. TRUE. Alcohol affects our brain, our central nervous system, and every part of our bodies. Even though we do not think of alcohol as a "drug", it is.
2. An athlete could lose up to two weeks training from getting drunk one time. TRUE. John Underwood's studies reveal that an athlete can lose up to two weeks of training effect by one night of intoxication.
3. People who drink or use drugs are more likely to be injured. TRUE. An NCAA study reveals that athletes who drink are more likely to suffer an injury (54%) than those who don't (26%).
4. Marijuana is harmless. FALSE. There are many misconceptions about marijuana. It is not a harmless drug. For example, a recent study by Harvard Medical School established that young people (and young brains!) who use marijuana experience a much higher likelihood of suffering from psychoses and other mental illnesses. Marijuana is also the leading non-alcoholic intoxicant in auto fatalities. While marijuana may relax some people and make them feel good, it is not harmless. What are the short-term effects of marijuana? Short-term effects include problems with memory and learning, distorted perception (sights, sounds, time, touch), trouble with thinking and problem solving, loss of motor coordination, increased heart rate, and anxiety. These effects are even greater when other drugs are mixed with weed. A user may also experience dry mouth and throat.

What are the long-term effects of marijuana? Marijuana smoke contains some of the same cancer-causing compounds as tobacco, sometimes in higher concentrations. Studies show that someone who smokes five joints per week may be taking in as many cancer-causing chemicals as someone who smokes a full pack of cigarettes every day.
Source: *The Partnership at drugfree.org*

5. Taking prescription drugs that belong to someone else is a safe and effective way to deal with pain. FALSE. Taking medications that do not belong to you is dicey. Statistics from the Oklahoma Bureau of Narcotics show that far more people die from prescription drug overdose (81%) than from street drug overdose (19%)

6. The ten most dangerous years of life are ages 14-24. TRUE. We lose more people to accidental deaths during this time than any other age group. Most of those deaths are due to car accidents, and most of those car accidents involve alcohol or other drugs.

7. On average, teens take their first drink at age 12. TRUE. Young people have greater access to alcohol than ever before. That access comes from store owners who are no vigilant about checking identifications, older friends who furnish alcohol to minors and even parents who foolishly think they should provide alcohol to their kids to "teach them to drink responsibly". Regular drinking, in which teens drink at least once a month, starts at around age 16. What is most troubling about these numbers is that many of these kids are drinking at excessive levels. Young people who begin drinking before age 15 (early onset drinking) are five times as likely to develop alcohol dependence and are more than twice as likely to become abusers of alcohol as those who begin drinking after age 21. (NSDUH Report)

8. Alcohol and other drugs interfere with messages your brain sends to your muscles. TRUE. The program Life of An Athlete shows how that interference occurs and how it hurts athletic performance.

9. My decisions about using alcohol or other drugs should be left up to me because I am the only one affected. FALSE.

The stories in this book and the Life of An Athlete program shows how a person's use of alcohol and other drugs is like a rock thrown in the pond. It adversely affects family, friends and even strangers who an intoxicated person may meet while driving on the roadway.

10. Children who have regular sit down meals with their family are 50% less likely to use alcohol or drugs. TRUE. The National Center on Addiction and Substance Abuse at Columbia University has performed studies and surveys that establish this fact. CASA Columbia's 2011 family dinner study finds that, compared to teens who have frequent family dinners (five to seven per week), those who have infrequent family dinners (fewer than three per week) are almost four times likelier to use tobacco; more than twice as likely to use alcohol; two-and-a-half times likelier to use marijuana; and almost four times likelier to say they expect to try drugs in the future.

If you drink alcohol from eight to midnight, for how long might you still have traces of alcohol in your system?

- 12 hours
- 24 hours
- 48 hours
- 4-5 days
- 3-8 weeks

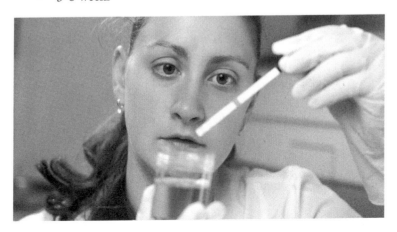

Answer: 4-5 days and 3-8 weeks

There are two possible answers to this one. Studies have shown that traces of alcohol may be found in urine four or five days after drinking one beer.

Traces of alcohol may be found in blood three to eight weeks after drinking. *Source: American Athletic Institute*

A Night Of Drinking

Here's a timeline to learn how alcohol affects your system over 19 hours after a night of drinking.

- (8PM) The evening starts at 8 PM. Over the course of the next four hours, you will have consumed 10 beers.
- (Midnight) You stop drinking at midnight. Even before that you reached the legal limit for Blood Alcohol Concentration (BAC), which measures the amount of alcohol in your body. **
- (Between Midnight and 2 AM) Even though you have stopped drinking, your BAC continues to rise over the next two hours.
- (2 AM) At 2 AM your blood alcohol concentration has finally reached its peak and starts to go down.
- (4 AM) Although your BAC is still coming down, you are still over the legal limit for DWI.
- (8 AM) 12 hours have passed since you started drinking, and you are still over the legal limit. It would be foolish to try to drive under these circumstances.
- (10 AM) It's 10 AM. You wake up with a hangover. You feel horrible, and breakfast doesn't look too appetizing. You're still legally intoxicated.
- (Noon) It's been a full 12 hours since you stopped drinking, you are no longer considered legally drunk; however, you could still be charged with a DWI because alcohol is still in your system.
- (4 PM) 19 hours after you started drinking, your blood alcohol level is back to where it was when you started drinking. (You probably don't feel much like going to practice to condition.)

Decreased Physical Capacities Related To Heavy Alcohol Consumption

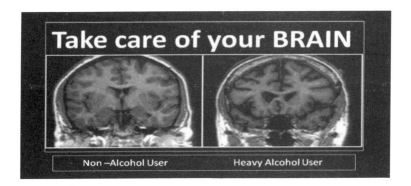

Brain Atrophy

The black area shown in this scan represents the space between your brain and the surrounding skull. If you drink heavily all the time, your brain actually shrinks in size.

It's similar to what a broken arm is like after six to eight weeks of non-use while in a cast. The arm loses muscle tone, becomes weaker and has visibly shrunk.

Source: Amen Clinics; www.amenclinics.com

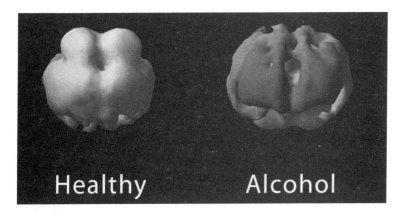

Decreased Brain Activity

The spaces shown here are not holes in your brain. They are areas of decreased brain activity. Note the damage that has been done to the brain of someone who is a heavy weekend alcohol user.

Speed

A study conducted with adult football players showed that alcohol drinkers had diminished performance in all modes of speed:

These are the most important kinds of speed you have that give you the edge on an opponent whether you are on offense of defense.

Startup speed (0-10 yards) - Speed needed to push off from the starting blocks

↓ 8%

Breakaway or acceleration speed (0-20 yards) - Speed needed to get by or go around someone

↓ 6%

Agility

Decrease in the ability to move side to side, which is necessary for avoiding a tackle in football or making a sudden directional change in sports like soccer, volleyball and tennis.

Side-to-side or lateral agility capabilities.

↓ 6%

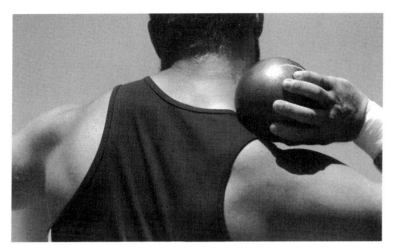

Explosive power and force

Weakening in the ability needed to push off in order to dunk a basketball or sprint out of the starting blocks.

↓11%

Power endurance

Lactic acid levels (the substance that makes our muscle fatigue and feel heavy and slow) will increase, greatly affecting performance. As a result, the ability to maintain speed over time, such as in distance running, or the number of bench press reps when lifting weights is lowered.

Loss of power endurance over time.

↓9%

Injury rate

Studies have shown that the injury rate is twice as high for athletes who drink than for non-drinkers.

- **54.8%** for drinkers
- **23.4%** for non-drinkers

(NCAA Football Injury Rate Study)

Sickness

Your immune capability is compromised if you drink alcohol. Because athletes stress their bodies, they are more prone to sickness than people who aren't athletes.

Reaction time

Alcohol affects reaction time (to both sight and sound) and hand eye coordination (two of the most important functions in any sport) up to 12 hours after consumption.

Psychological factors

Use of alcohol lowers motivation, focus, ability to control distractions, levels of expectation and arousal. These are the factors needed to think on your feet, anticipate and keep your mind on the game.

Total Physical Performance Lost

11.4% FOR ELITE (OLYMPIC LEVEL) ATHLETES
15.0% FOR COLLEGE ATHLETES
30.0% FOR HIGH SCHOOL ATHLETES

Athletes remain one of the highest "at risk" groups for drug and alcohol abuse. Do you know why? Athletes train hard, work hard, and are naturally competitive. Most athletes –and most young people--are willing to take risks. Especially if a friend or a group of friends encourage them to take that risk.

Athletes tend to hang out with other athletes. When they win... it's time to celebrate. And when they lose... they feel the need to blow off steam. Alcohol and other drugs are often involved in both of these situations.

Peer pressure is something every young person knows about.

There's negative peer pressure like Brandon Whitten experienced—pressure to party, experiment with drugs, to drink or to take some pills.

But there's also positive peer pressure where you can make a difference in the life of your friends and teammates by making smart decisions about alcohol or other drugs and encouraging others to do the same.

It's your choice to make the right decision. You get to choose your fate.

Here's NFL player Chris Chamberlain who attended high school in Bethany, Oklahoma and played college football at the University of Tulsa. Chris is going to talk with you about the influence of positive peer pressure on the Bethany State Championship football team.

Chris Chamberlain

My name is Chris Chamberlain, and I play linebacker for the New Orleans Saints.

As I've been a part of many teams in my career, I find that one person who is passionate and positive can affect those around them.

In high school, I was fortunate to play quarterback, free-safety and win a state championship. We had seen in previous years how the abuse of alcohol and other drugs had hurt our team, and we thought that we would have a chance to go further in playoffs and win more games. So we came up with the idea that we wanted to sign a pledge—to not drink, to not smoke, or do any of those things that might hinder our chances on the field. We all signed it, and those of us that didn't have a problem with alcohol gave up soda. So we'd be sacrificing and giving up something like everyone else.

It's something that I don't think has ever been done at the school, and we got a State Championship—something that had never been done before.

By us group of Seniors presenting this pledge and committing ourselves to do this, we affected not only ourselves but really had a positive influence on all of our teammates around us.

So, you, sitting there at home may be faced with this decision right now. Are you going to go along with the partiers and are you going to fall into that lifestyle, or are you going to be disciplined and obedient and do what you need to do to give yourself the best chance to succeed?

I'm Chris Chamberlain. What's YOUR fate?

View Video

Charles Howell

All of us have to make decisions about how we are going to live our lives. You can make poor decisions and use alcohol and other drugs, or you can make good decisions to live a healthy life style. Listen to what Oklahoma State grad and PGA golfer Charles Howell has to say about making decisions.

My name is Charles Howell and I play golf on the PGA tour. I was always attracted to the fact that it's an individual game, that I'm my own coach, my own boss, my own mentor if you will. I got all the credit, but with that, I got all the blame.

The game of golf as many of you all know, is the only professional sport in which the players call penalties on themselves. So in an instance in my rookie year on the PGA tour, I'm playing; I'll never forget. It was actually in Dallas at the Byron Nelson. As we all know, it can get quite windy in Dallas, and I set my putter-head down behind the ball, and the ball oscillated just slightly. Nobody ever would have known, nobody ever would have seen it. And I had to call the penalty on myself.

Just to clarify and bring things in perspective, the first place just for that tournament was a million dollars, and in golf, trust me, every stroke counts. That being my rookie year, I had to make as much money as possible to earn my status or earn my job on the PGA tour, so that one stroke could've been the difference in a million dollars, it could've been the difference in having a job or not having a job. There were plenty of motives in there for me not to call the penalty on myself.

Golf is a game of character. There are so many parallels to the game of golf, and the game of life. And I know that I'm my own boss. Just as that, I've made a decision to stay free of drugs and alcohol. It's right there, it's available, and it's not always the easiest decision to make, the easiest call to make. But remember you are your own boss just as I'm my own boss on the golf-course, and you can make that decision. You know, it's very easy for big decisions to be made where there are a lot of people around, where your parents are around, or your mentors are around; it's easy to make the right call then. The biggest decisions in life are, more times than not, decisions nobody ever sees but you. And just knowing that you are accountable to yourself in that quiet moment. In that quiet moment, when you're by yourself, it's just you, and "I could just try it one time. What is this like?" Just know that if you can make that decision and be strong that one time, just know that it will be easier the next time and easier the next time. And then it won't even be a discussion.

I'm Charles Howell. I play golf on the PGA tour.
What's YOUR fate?

View Video

Young Person's Decision Making Exercise

What's the best thing I can do to make good decisions about alcohol or other drugs?

1. Just use your will power
2. Tell your parents to constantly nag you
3. Don't hang with others who misuse alcohol or other drugs

Correct answer: 3

The single best thing you can do is to not hang around people who drink or use other kinds of drugs. Most young athletes who hang out with people who drink or use drugs are going to end up drinking or using. It also helps to have a friend that you partner with. Find someone who wants to make good decisions and reinforce each other. Encourage each other. Call each other if you're having a problem. Who you hang with is the number one thing that determines what kinds of choices you make about alcohol and drugs.

What should I do if I see underage drinking or drugs at a party?
1. Just leave
2. Stay around and use your will power to resist
3. Yell out to everyone "I'm calling the police!"

Correct answer: 1

The best thing to do is leave immediately and take as many friends with you as you can. Underage drinking and illegal use of drugs is against the law. If the police arrive, you could go to jail even if you aren't drinking or using. This is not a time for compromise or allowing your friends to talk you into staying. You wouldn't stick around if a rattlesnake slithered into the party.

What Do I Say To Friends Who Pressure Me To Drink Or Use Other Drugs?

1. "Not now, maybe later."
2. "I'm not that kind of person."
3. "No way. I learned that stuff wipes out all the training I've been putting in."

Correct answer: 3

Actually, if any of these responses works, use it. But the best answer is to talk about what you've learned in the Life of An Athlete program. Using hurts performance. Also remember, friends who pressure you into drinking or using drugs are not really your friends. Make up your mind ahead of time what you're going to say or do and picture yourself saying it. Rehearse it in your mind. Something like: "I'm not doing that because I've learned how much it hurts my athletic performance." If they keep pressuring you, leave and start looking for some new friends.

What If One Of My Friends Passes Out From Drinking Or Using Drugs?

1. Leave them and let them sleep it off
2. Let an adult know right away or call 911
3. Check their pulse and breathing every hour but don't bother them

Correct answer: 2

Never leave a friend who has passed out from drinking or taking drugs, even if you think you might get in trouble. Many young people have died because their friends left them alone thinking they would "sleep it off". If your friend has passed out or is looking or acting very sick, call 911 or get an adult involved who can help.

What if I'm having trouble with my current alcohol or drug use and want help?

1. Talk to your parents or an adult you trust.
2. Call or email FATE
3. Check out the resources at the end of this program
4. All of the above

Correct answer: 4

How Your Brain Works

Everything you do as an athlete starts right up here — in your brain.

In order for your brain to work at optimal levels, there are three requirements:

It must be rested, it must have sufficient blood sugar levels, and it cannot be affected by alcohol or other drugs.

Notice that I said "alcohol and OTHER drugs". That's because alcohol IS a drug. It affects your body and brain chemistry. Most people don't think about alcohol as being a drug—but it is—and, it affects your body and your brain.

The brain sends messages or impulses to your muscles. Alcohol and other drugs interfere with the messages between your brain and your muscles. When you use alcohol or take drugs, the proper movements — or biomechanics — needed for sports performance get interrupted. Your athletic performance and school work suffer when you use alcohol or other drugs.

We used to think that most brain development took place during the first 3 to 5 years of life. Recent studies, however, show that more brain development occurs from age 13 until age 21 than the entire first 13 years of your life.

During those years, the parts of your brain that help with making good, smart decisions are going through a critical growth period.

Parts of the brain associated with athletic abilities are also being perfected during this time. Unfortunately, the damage caused by alcohol and drug use may be lifelong — and irreversible. In other words, using alcohol or other drugs is like pouring sand into the machinery of your brain.

The areas of pink represent brain activity. That's a good thing! Notice how much brain activity is generated by a non-alcohol user versus a heavy alcohol user at age15.

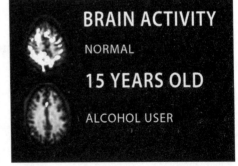

Your brain has to work harder to do less.

The skills you learn early in your athletic career are stored in a very small part of your brain.

Once you master a skill, such as shooting a free throw or swinging a tennis racket, the skill stays with you.

It's called skill cataloging or skill acquisition. Through practice and repetition, the skill becomes automatic, and you do it the same every time.

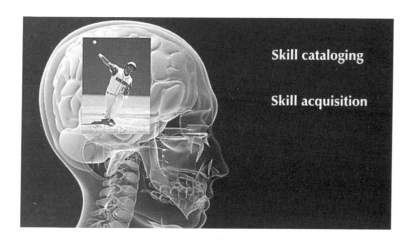

A good example of this is throwing a baseball. The timing and techniques you use to get the ball where you want it are recalled from the cataloged part of your brain.

A heavy alcohol user must use more brain energy to perform the same actions.

Checkout this image; as you can see, the person's brain that has been subjected to alcohol use is using more brain energy for the same motion.

Alcohol and other drugs are so taxing on your central nervous system because they block the ability to send signals from the place where you learned a skill to where you need it to perform the action.

The brain has to rewire itself to compensate for damage caused by alcohol and other drugs.

Listen to what Gerald McCoy has to say about how he dealt with temptations to use alcohol and other drugs and the effect it can have on your training.

Gerald McCoy

I'm Gerald McCoy, Defensive Tackle for the Tampa Bay Buccaneers.

I started playing football when I was 7 years old. But around 9, 10 years old I got serious about it when I realized I actually had a little bit of talent. I wasn't going to let anything get in my way. That included drugs, alcohol, things of that sort. Didn't touch it. Stayed away from it. Wasn't a part of my life, because I knew it would do nothing but slow me down.

I grew up on south side of Oklahoma City, so those types of things take place. I mean, right up the street where my school was. It was like, I mean, you see people on the street sorta doing deals. You know, you're leaving school, you gotta drive past these certain deals, and these places—and you know what goes on in there. So I was around it all the time. My friends kinda tapped into that world early, from middle school all the way up through high school. And it was tough for me to still be those guys friend and not get involved with those types of things, but I had a goal in mind.

I know, as a competitor, as an athlete, you don't want to let anybody else have an edge over you. And drugs and alcohol give that person that edge. When you use drugs and alcohol, it affects your performance, not just for the next day, not just for the day after that, not just for the day after that—it can affect you up to two weeks. It doesn't matter what types of gifts God's blessed you with, what type of athlete you are, this person's always going to have this edge on you because you're slowing yourself down. This thing you're doing is a quick sensation. It's gonna eventually go away, and then if things don't work out as far as your career, your future, that's long term. And you look back on the things you did, the decisions you made, and those few nights you had or those few weekends or those few months—it's not worth ruining your career. It's not worth throwing away your career or your goals just for a good time.

I'm Gerald McCoy. What's YOUR fate?

View Video

When you're in top physical condition nerve impulses from your brain are telling your muscles what to do. ALL your body systems are working together as they should be. These systems can be negatively impacted when alcohol or drugs are added. Let's take a tour of the human body to learn more.

VISION
How does alcohol negatively impact vision?

The ability to track and follow moving objects is critical in most sports. Alcohol decreases this capacity in the visual system making it difficult to maintain focus making it difficult to keep your eye on the ball or follow your opponent's movements.

LUNGS AND OXYGEN INTAKE
How does alcohol negatively impact the lungs?

With exercise your lungs try to get oxygen to your working muscles and clear carbon dioxide (CO_2) out of your system.

Alcohol makes this very difficult. Less breathing means less O_2 and more CO_2. As a result, your muscles begin to suffocate. You experience a decrease in speed, power and endurance.

When the lungs are infected or injured, heavy alcohol consumption can increase the susceptibility of pneumonia or acute respiratory distress.

HEART
How does alcohol negatively the heart?

Mild use of alcohol can be harmful to some people and heavy use is certainly harmful. Long-term and excessive alcohol use can raise your blood pressure to an unhealthy level, sometimes resulting in stroke or death. Recent studies reveal that 19% of youth now have high blood pressure, and alcohol raises your blood pressure even further!

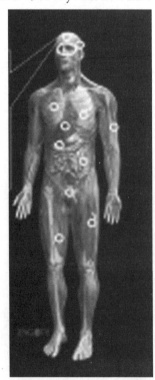

Alcohol pushes your heart rate higher and over time the amount of blood your heart can pump out will decrease.

Oxygen rich blood will be unable reach your working muscles causing you to slow down and become weaker.

Alcohol also affects your heart beat rhythm.

LIVER
How does alcohol negatively impact the liver?

The liver filters the body of poisons and makes muscle fuels called glycogen.

Alcohol is a metabolic poison, which your liver must deal with before it will make fuels for your muscles.

As result, you will run out of muscle fuels early causing muscle fatigue.

Chronic and long-term alcohol use can inflict severe damage to the liver. Alcoholic liver disease (ALD) takes various forms including cirrhosis, which is the most serious and final form of the disease.

FAST / SLOW TWITCH MUSCLES
How does alcohol negatively impact fast and slow twitch muscles?

Fast twitch muscles are called into play with explosive movements such as heavy lifting or sprinting. This is anaerobic exercise, meaning the muscles don't require oxygen to do their work. A substance called creatine increases the work output in fast muscle fibers. Prolonged alcohol use, however, works against any benefits gained by creatine.

Slow twitch muscle fibers are aerobic, meaning they require oxygen to generate force. These muscles are called into play for long distance running

MUSCLE REPAIR
How does alcohol negatively impact muscle repair?

Your ability to repair damaged muscle is reduced.

When we train, muscle becomes damaged. We repair it by making protein into new fibers. Drinking slows down this repair process. This process is most reduced in your speed and power muscles.

HGH HUMAN GROWTH HORMONE
How does alcohol negatively impact Human Growth Hormone?

Human Growth Hormone (HGH) is the second most important hormone an athlete has for repairing damaged muscle. Normal HGH output keeps a certain amount of muscle on your skeleton and allows you to burn fuels for physical work. You reduce HGH output by about 70% if you drink heavily.

Source: American Athletic Institute

MUSCLE FUELS AND ENERGY SYSTEMS
How does alcohol negatively impact muscle fuels and energy systems?

When you finish a workout or competition, you have little or no fuels left in the muscles. Normally, we can reload our muscles with fuels in 8-12 hours. After drinking alcohol, it can take 16-24 hours for the body to reload muscle fuels (glycogen).

STRESS HORMONE
How does alcohol negatively impact the release of cortisol?

Two triangular glands, called adrenal glands, sit on the top of each kidney, and among other things, produce cortisol (the stress hormone) and epinephrine (adrenaline), which once released, speed up heart rate, blood pressure, and other bodily functions that help you cope with stress.

Alcohol greatly increases the release of cortisol. Higher and more prolonged levels of cortisol can interfere with the body's ability to recover from a workout or game which can lead to poor athletic performance, lowered immunity and can undo some of the benefits gained during training.

TESTOSTERONE
How does alcohol negatively impact testosterone levels?

Everything you do as an athlete—both men and women—is determined by testosterone.

Alcohol decreases testosterone to levels that do not support gains in training effect or condition for up to 96 hours (four days) after heavy drinking.

Basically, you are at practice, but the hormones you need to gain training effect and condition are not sufficient. You practice but no improvement comes. Your opponents are pulling away from you.

Males have ten times as much testosterone as females. Drinking alcohol causes testosterone levels to go down. Some teen males who drink and train heavily have testosterone levels similar to girls. Girls who drink are even more susceptible to the damaging effects of alcohol, because they have less testosterone to begin with.

Making healthy lifestyle decisions will have a positive impact on your athletic performance and your life. When you exercise, you lose water through sweat from your tissues, including your muscles and your brain.

If the fluid is not replenished, your athletic performance and health will suffer.

Alcohol is not an effective way to replenish fluids. Alcohol consumption raises the rate of urination, which depletes water and essential vitamins from the body.

The morning after heavy drinking, the body sends a desperate message to replenish its water supply - usually manifested in the form of an extremely dry mouth. Headaches result from dehydration, because the body's organs try to make up for their own water loss by stealing water from the brain, causing the brain to decrease in size and pull on the membranes that connect the brain to the skull, resulting in pain.

While a strong cup of coffee may wake you up, it is not a good way to hydrate. Caffeine acts as a diuretic, causing fluids to be drawn away from muscle tissues, leading to cramps and muscle pulls.

Energy drinks don't help with hydration either. In fact, they can cause overstimulation of the central nervous system, which eventually results in chronic fatigue. Energy drinks actually limit the ability to maintain high level mental or physical performance rather than increase it.

You need water before, during and after exercise to replenish lost fluids.

Most of us have seen on television, on the internet or read about the use of prescription drugs, the use of steroids by athletes and the use of marijuana.

Recently, our state suffered the loss of an outstanding college athlete because of lethal combination of prescription drugs. Sometimes, athletes use these drugs to make pain go away. That's what Brandon Whitten was trying to do.

Sometimes, drugs are used to try and increase performance or bulk up. And sometimes, they're used because people think it's exciting and fun to experiment, and that there is no big danger involved.   But the truth you need to know is taking or smoking these drugs is very dangerous and can have fatal consequences. Taking prescription drugs that have not been prescribed for you is like picking up a rattlesnake that you thought was a garter snake. And contrary to what you may have been told, steroids can affect you in ways that are dangerous and irreversible. Even smoking marijuana is not as risk free as you may have been led to believe. Take a look at the following information about prescription drugs, steroids and marijuana. You may be surprised by what you learn.

SOMETIMES YOUR CHOICES HAVE A HOOK

(1) IS ALCOHOL A "DRUG"?

Yes, alcohol is a drug.

Alcohol can affect every organ in the human body - brain, liver, stomach and heart to name a few

Although alcohol is not a prescription drug or an illegal substance (for adults), it carries all the risks of addiction and illness that street drugs do.

Your brain runs your body

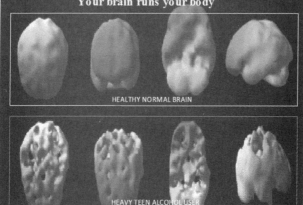

HEALTHY NORMAL BRAIN

HEAVY TEEN ALCOHOL USER

Scans by Amen Clinics

(2) TRUE OR FALSE?

GETTING HIGH ON PRESCRIPTION DRUGS IS SAFER THAN TAKING STREET DRUGS

FALSE

There is a perception that use and abuse of Rx drugs is "safer" than other drugs or even alcohol but it's not true!

STEROIDS: DANGER!

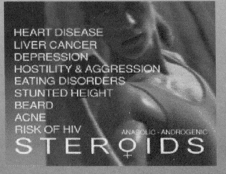

HEART DISEASE
LIVER CANCER
DEPRESSION
HOSTILITY & AGGRESSION
EATING DISORDERS
STUNTED HEIGHT
BEARD
ACNE
RISK OF HIV

ANABOLIC · ANDROGENIC

S T E R O I D S

1x DRUNK = 14 DAYS LOST TRAINING EFFECT

DON'T TOSS YOUR TRAINING TIME

(3) True or False?
Marijuana is a harmless drug
Answer: FALSE

Fact: Marijuana smoking affects the brain and leads to impaired short-term memory, perception, judgment, and motor skills.

We can't overemphasize the importance of training to athletic performance. Effective training requires dedication, focus and time. Time matters and people waste a lot of it.

Back in the 1950s, a Russian scientist named Leo Matveev said, "You can't achieve in competition what you haven't achieved in training."

How do you think you will measure up to someone who has put more effort and focus into training?

Matveev also said, "When you're not training, somewhere someone IS training, and when you meet them, they will beat you."

Between competitions and training sessions your body and your brain need time to recharge and heal. If you're pushing the envelope, you're stressing your body. That puts you at risk for injuries and decreases the ability of your immune system to fight sickness.

Adequate sleep and good nutrition are essential to good athletic performance and must be factored into every training regimen.

After a night of heavy drinking, a hangover is the least of your problems. You're still messed up for several days afterward.

How much do you really lose as an athlete when you party?

A muscle study that was done by the American Athletic Institute showed that you could lose up to 14 days of training effect every time you get drunk.

Think about it.

You just took 14 steps backward instead of 14 steps forward. You train but you don't get any better. It's a waste of everything you set out to do.

You get to choose your fate—for today and for the future. You can use alcohol or other drugs and lose. Or you can abstain and gain.

Are you really at your best or just some shadow of what you could be? If you drink alcohol or use other drugs, you are giving away your talent ... giving away your game.

If your teammates drink alcohol or use drugs your team is giving away your chance to succeed at your best.

Here's the bottom line from studies conducted by Olympic trainer and coach John Underwood, the total physical performance lost by elite world-class athletes when they used alcohol or other drugs is 11.4%. Just think, if some of the top athletes in the world lose 11.4% from their performance, how much would a middle school, high school or college athlete lose? For sure it would be much more. It is not unrealistic to think that it might be as much as a 15% to a 30% loss of total performance potential. How would you like to improve to a whole new level as an individual or together as a team?

Individual decisions affect group outcomes. Are you all at your best?

Chances are your athletic career will end after you leave high school.

Approximately 2% of high school athletes go on to play college sports and of those who play in college only about 2% will ever become professionals in a sport. That's a very small number.

So while sports are important, you need to think about what else is going on in your life. How are you making decisions? Who are you letting influence you? Are you a positive influence on others? And who will be affected by the choices you make concerning alcohol or other drugs? Your family? Your friends? Your coaches and teammates?

Unlike TV, there are no replays in life. The decisions you make about alcohol and other drugs affect not only you. They affect those around you.

Brandon's decisions affected not only HIS life, but changed the life of his family and friends forever.

We hope you've learned something about alcohol and other drugs and how they affect your life as an athlete. Participating in athletics is fun. There's the rush of competition, camaraderie, the feeling of accomplishment and recognition. Experience it fully. Enjoy it. There's nothing like it. But as you enjoy it, think about the decisions you're making along the way.

Your decisions affect your fate. So as you think about your fate, think about the impact the decisions you make today will have in the future, on you as well as on your family and friends. The good news is you can choose your fate. You can make the decision to LIVE THE LIFE OF AN ATHLETE. The choice to make good decisions is yours, and we hope this program will help you make the right decisions.

CHAPTER EIGHT
Stories Change Lives

In our FATE programs, we utilize videos and stories from our athlete friends. We believe that stores have the power to change people's lives. We draw courage and hope and inspiration from stories and we learn that people can and do make good choices about alcohol and other drugs. Here are some additional stories that will inspire and motivate you.

Roy Williams

Roy Williams, former University of Oklahoma and NFL football star.

I'm Roy Williams. Drug and alcohol abuse could've affected my life, but I chose to go another route. In life, you have choices, decisions, then after your decisions, you have consequences.

I was playing a game called the Red River Shootout—Oklahoma versus Texas in the Cotton Bowl. The stadium was split, and you have all these fans going crazy yelling.

It was the fourth quarter, everybody's screaming, the fans, you know. Texas quarterback Chris Simms is doing his cadence about to snap the ball. My heart was beating fast, and I knew that I would make the play. Something spoke to me and said, "Roy, jump." The play happened so fast, I jumped, knocked the ball out of Chris's hands, and my teammate, Teddy Lehman, was right there to intercept the pass, seal the deal and walk the ball in the end zone. That's how the Superman play became the Superman play because I made the decision to jump. That decision, the end result, helped us to win.

Sometimes, making the right decision will help you win in life. That play, with all those distractions, is just like when kids at school are asking you to try things like drinking and smoking dope. But you're staying on the straight and narrow; you have your mind on what you want to do in life, on what you want to do that day. You're not going to let anything distract you, because you have a goal in mind. The, just like the Superman play, boom! It happens. I jump, I make the play, everybody's cheering, everybody's excited. But sometimes, when you're making these decisions about alcohol and drugs, nobody will be cheering for you. But inside you know that you made the right choice, that you turned something down when normally other kids don't. Sometimes when you make the right decision, nobody's going be cheering, but you know that you made the right decision.

You have to ask yourself, do I want to partake with my friends using drugs, weed, alcohol, and pills? Or do I want to make the right decision?

I'm Roy Williams. What's your FATE?

View Video

Keiton Page

Keiton Page, former Oklahoma State University basketball star.

I'm Keiton Page. I played basketball for four years at Oklahoma State as a starting point guard, and I had the opportunity to become a coach at Oklahoma State after my college career ended. As a player, I made the NCAA tournament twice. I hold the record at Oklahoma State for the most minutes ever played, and I rank number one in three-pointers made. It was the best four years of my life, and that's the main thing I want to say to young athletes: the temptations are going to be there. They're going to be out there, and yeah, they'll be tough at times, but the decision to say no always leads to a better future.

Growing up in a basketball family, my brother was a basketball player and my dad was his basketball coach. My goal was to play here at Oklahoma State, and so that's what motivated me, always just being in the gym and just trying to get to, trying to elevate my game to a level where I could eventually, one day, play here at Oklahoma State.

I always had the keys to the gym, my dad being a basketball coach. That's all I ever wanted to do, was be in the gym. Most nights of the week I was up there by myself, just putting up as many shots as I could. You have to have something that motivates you to be in there doing it by yourself, and playing here at Oklahoma State was what was motivating me.

Growing up in high school and being a good athlete, there are always temptations. There are always the people that present you with drugs, alcohol and that sort of thing. That's just one thing I knew was an easy decision for me, to say no. It was an easy decision for me to back away from that because I knew the goal I had ahead of me and that was to play college basketball here at Oklahoma State.

I think for any young athlete to reach the level that you want to get to, that's the kind of things that you have to say no to. The decisions you make will affect your future. Growing up, you play with numerous, numerous talented guys. There's been several that I've played with, high school through college, that have let off the court issues—temptations—not let them reach their full potential. It's a sad thing to see because some of these guys are some of the top guys in the country. They could be making tons of money playing, and they let the off court issues or temptations, such as drug and alcohol, get to them, and they never reach that full potential.

It's your decision whether or not you want to get in there and put the countless hours in when nobody's looking. It's your decision if you want to let the temptations get to you and not reach your full ability.

I'm Keiton Page. What's your FATE?

View Video

Mark Clayton

Mark Clayton, former University of Oklahoma and NFL football star.

My name is Mark Clayton, a member of the St. Louis Rams.

My real dad struggled with alcohol and drug abuse. He went to jail and suffered the consequences from that, and our family was broken. To see my dad do those sorts of things, that was a let down, because you know, that's your dad. I guess as a kid, for most kids, they probably look at their dad as the hero or the man or the dude, like you look up to your dad. Unfortunately, with my dad, it was a continuous let down after let down after let down.

I went on to college at Oklahoma University to play football. When I first got to college it was really just about enjoying myself. I got drunk for the first time at college, and after that I got drunk occasionally. I tried marijuana in college and did that for a little bit. If I'd made the decision to continue doing drugs, whether that was marijuana or alcohol, I can guarantee you I would not have been playing in the NFL.

Our society is tough because everything is so accessible and people want to grow up so fast. They want to be adults, they want to be grown, or they say "I am grown, and I know what I'm doing". They think I can choose to do what I want with my body, when I want, with whoever I want, however I want. That's what I'm going to do. And that is ridiculous.

Every drink you take, you're knocking years out. Every smoke, every sniff, snort, whatever it is, you're knocking years off your life. No matter what it is you're knocking years off your life. You can go out and kill yourself, straight up or kill somebody else, and then who you're really hurting and wrecking is everybody you're connected to, everybody that loves you, and it's very selfish.

Don't feel like you're above, that you don't have to listen to nobody that's ahead of you because you got it figured out. Some people say, "It's a new day, a new time, and this is how it is now." Nah. It ain't changed. Alcohol killed then and it kills now. Drugs killed then, and they kill now. It ain't no different.

I'm Mark Clayton. What's your FATE?

View Video

Brandon Mason, All American wrestler.

I'm Brandon Mason, a former Oklahoma State wrestler, and I am now a medical student at OSU.

I wrestled at Lewis Central High School in Council Bluffs, Iowa and ended up being a three time state champion there and had a high school record of 195-2.

In high school, I had people to look up to. Two brothers, Trent and Travis Paulson, were world team members for wrestling, and they're people that kind of kept me on that straight path to do the right thing. There were also those in high school who wanted you to go out drinking on the weekends, even though it was in the season. When you're faced with those kinds of decisions, you have to weigh your options, what you want to do. With the goals I had, I knew I shouldn't be doing that stuff.

I accepted a scholarship to come wrestle at Oklahoma State for the Cowboys. When I got to college, it was the same thing—people wanting you to go to parties on the weekend. I had mentors that were on the team that were multiple time national champions that didn't go out on the weekends, so I knew I shouldn't be doing that either.

I made a commitment that during wrestling season that I would stay away from alcohol even when I was of age. I think sacrifices are important; the science shows that you will perform better if you abstain. But also knowing that you've made the sacrifice to stay away from those substances, it gives you a little edge I believe. You know that you're giving something up for something greater and something better.

I had goals to be a successful division one wrestler. . I ended up an All-American in 2006 at 174 pounds. I got fifth place at nationals. I also had goals to get into medical school afterwards, and now I'm in med school. And because I had those goals, I knew that the short term enjoyments of alcohol and drugs weren't for me.

I'm Brandon Mason. I'm an All-American wrestler at Oklahoma State University, and a medical student. What's your FATE?

View Video

Billy Bajema

Billy Bajema, former Oklahoma State University football and NFL player.

I'm Billy Bajema; I play in the NFL.

I grew up playing all kinds of sports: football, baseball, basketball. Just whatever season it was, I was going to playing some sport. I got to the point when I was nine or ten years old where I started setting goals and deciding I would love to be a professional athlete someday.

It was around that time that I decided to make a commitment to never let a drug or alcohol enter my body. I didn't see any sense in going so hard for something and then taking two steps forward and one step back.

In high school, I had opportunities to go to parties where there was not going to be really anything to do except for drink, doing things that I knew I didn't want to be a part of. College is an even bigger challenge to stay focused. You've got so many things, especially as a college athlete, thrown at you. So developing your identity, standing firm in your goals, and the things that you want to do as a college student is really important.

I think the moment I made the team with the San Francisco 49ers, my first year in the NFL, and going into the locker room the first game, seeing my last name on the back of the jersey and my own locker, that moment it all kind of came to me, and it was exciting.

It's important to decide who you want to be, to set your goals and figure out what you want to do. And you've got to make a decision and a commitment to stay away from drugs, to stay away from alcohol because nobody wants to end up down the road that drugs and alcohol take you.

I'm Billy Bajema. What's your FATE?

View Video

Curtis Lofton

Curtis Lofton, former University of Oklahoma and NFL football star.

I'm Curtis Lofton, and I play linebacker for the New Orleans Saints in the NFL.

Pretty much my whole life, as I grew up, my mother was in and out of prison doing drugs, drinking alcohol. That left me and my brothers to live with my grandmother. Which was kind of for the best because my grandma...she's a great lady. But there were times where I wished my mom was at my game or wished she was at my graduation and stuff like that, but she wasn't there, and it hurt. But it made me who I am today.

Being in the NFL, you have to ask yourself what's going to be your advantage. Everyone's big, everyone's strong, everyone's fast. What's going to be your advantage? For me it starts on Monday. You know, I get into film. I study it, and once Sunday comes, once I see that and I know our defense and before the ball is even snapped, I limit it down to two plays; what it's going to be. So that's what allows me to play the way I do.

In the NFL, it's a matter of inches—making a tackle, making a catch—that's going to allow me to be the player that I am today. Life is definitely a game of inches; I wouldn't say inches, I would say decisions. You've got to make good decisions. You make one decision; it's going to affect your life. So every decision you make, just think about your future and how it's going to affect it.

If you're out drinking, smoking, doing drugs, whatever man, that's going to slow you down. It just tears up families and destroys people's lives. So just think everything that you want to accomplish in your life, all your goals. And if you're doing drugs, you're more than likely not going to accomplish any of those.

Curtis Lofton. Middle linebacker in the NFL.
What's your FATE?

View Video

CHAPTER NINE
John Underwood Speaks

John Underwood

I'm John Underwood, President of the American Athletic Institute. For the last 15 years I've been studying the effect of alcohol on athletic performance, and I've grown increasingly concerned about what's going on with young athletes.

About 2% of high school athletes become NCAA Athletes, and the NCAA data reflects a progression. When kids go to college, even more of them drink; more get caught up in it. Overall, about 80% of NCAA athletes use alcohol regularly in D1 and D2 programs, and marijuana is now heading for 1 out of 3 NCAA athletes. Last year at the NCAA championships, it was pretty common knowledge that the use rates for positive tests for marijuana went way up. What's been reported is there were three times the positive test rates at NCAA championships last year than ever before. Trends in marijuana use are so unacceptable that it's scary. Kids are actually saying now that marijuana's not as bad as alcohol. And it's a drug we can use and perform and get away with it. So we need to concentrate not just on alcohol but on marijuana and try to dispel some of these misconceptions.

Facing the issues

People are facing the issues for the first time in history—underage drinking, societally, was just a right of passage—this was just what kids did, we all did it, that kind of stuff. But now people know underage drinking has gone from the back-burner to the front-burner. And we have many, many more people concerned about it. We have new studies and brain scans, and that's how people realize, damage is damage, and if you damage the brain at a young age, you traumatize the brain for future possibilities.

Perspective on training the brain

We also try to give people perspective on training effect, and what's important. Look at your brain as the number one factor in athletic performance, because it is. Your brain and your central nervous system are by far more important than your heart, lungs, and muscles.

Importance of brain

Over the last decade, we've come to understand that there's something so much more important than your central system, your heart and lungs and your peripheral system, which are the muscles that do the work, and that's your central nervous system and your brain. There are so many things that can affect it. The biggest thing we've seen, we refer to it now as central nervous system readiness. If your brain or central nervous system have any glitches, it's not going to happen.

Body recovers quickly

We also know that when we do maximal training and maximal stress to the body, that muscles heart and lungs recover very quickly—24 hours maximum maybe 48 hour from maximal physical stress. The brain and central nervous system take much longer to recover. Something like 48 to 72 hours to recover. You have to take this into consideration. That's way more important than the other systems that can recover rapidly.

There are three outcomes to training: you can improve, stay the same or you can actually get worse. In training, we train speed, power, agility, reaction, endurance, which are those vital motor skills. We know how to train the human body, how much stress it can take, what kind of workouts make things happen, but we're now spending more time saying what we aren't doing that we could be doing. And one of the biggest factors that we're starting on, now that we haven't spent enough time trying to influence it, is lifestyle. What you do off the court, off the mat, off the playing field influences what you're trying to do out there.

Producing the positives

Any athlete who has the talent, puts in the time, effort, and energy, but is not living a lifestyle that's conducive to being successful, is basically throwing out all those positives. When we do what I call "explaining training, we explain in-depth to athletes the training, recovery, and adaptation triangle to make kids understand it's not just about doing a workout. It's about after the workout's over, recovering as quickly as possible so you can get adaptation, you can get the improvement. And that takes time. Way more of an investment than one workout.

So we explain to kids and young athletes training and recovery. That's a concept they need to hear. When you take alcohol into the equation, we're seeing recovery times now slowed to 3 or 4 days. So basically, you do a hard workout, you could be recovering in 24 hours, but instead we're seeing now 3 days, 4 days later until their back to a level where they can again make progress. For any athlete who wants to make progress, that's not how you make it. And for top athletes, when they hear this message, it's a very quick learning curve.

When we work with top athletes who really care about performance, elite athletes, Olympic athletes, navy seals, spec ops, and so forth, as soon as they hear this information, it comes into focus. Other athletes who are not as serious about performance, of course, can rationalize anything. They say, hey, I can do this and get away with it. And maybe it will get them the same performance they have now, but their progression of improvement will slow, level out, or not happen. They'll never be as good as they could have been.

In the many years we've been studying the effects of marijuana and alcohol on high level athletic performance, we haven't found any positive effects.

When I'm out speaking to coaches and athletes, I'll ask in a meeting, "Does anybody know of a positive effect that will help your performance by drinking or smoking pot?", and nobody responds. Because there are none.

We're talking about depressant drugs that shut down brain activity, and because we now understand the connection between brain and body, we know that if you shut down brain activity, you shut down body activity. The stress that alcohol and marijuana creates in your body is something that causes your brain to bypass every other stress in your body to deal with a metabolic poison or a toxin in your system. It's amazing how your body shuts off everything else it's doing until it gets rid of the toxic priority, which is the alcohol.

This all starts with drink number one. I think this is the thing that most people don't understand: the cascade of negative effects in the human body starts with drink number one. Hormones diminish starting with drink one. Testosterone diminishes with the first drink. You don't have to get drunk to suffer harmful effects on your athletic performance.

Advice to coaches

As far as coaches, the Life of An Athlete program offers a lot. It gives opportunities to discuss things that don't get discussed anymore, like lifestyle. The first pages in an athlete's playbook should be about lifestyle. The cornerstone of being an athlete is what you do on and off the field and that you're living your life in a way that sets you up to be successful.

A lot of coaches make statements like, "Drugs are bad. Don't do drugs." Coaches should tell athletes why they're bad, tell them what they do. And if you don't have the background to talk on that subject with your teams, the information's available now through Life of An Athlete. LOA provides information to coaches where you can say, "This is why I'm asking you not to be involved in this kind of stuff during your sport year."

Coaches underestimate impact they can have on young athletes. Even if you know you can have an impact, you underestimate it. These guys look up to you. We did a survey of 30,000 middle and high school athletes in New York State and asked them what the number one thing they wanted from their coach was, and you know what they said? They said they wanted their coach to be a role model. That's something for you coaches never to forget.

These young people spend more time with you than with their parents. You take them on trips, and you're with them a lot. You have a special relationship with these young people. Don't ever underestimate the impact you can have.

If you're a coach, you most likely had a coach that influenced your life. Maybe that's the reason you're even coaching today. Ask young people, "Who was the most important person besides your parents?" So many kids would say, "My coach." And it's usually a high school coach that impacted these kids at an impressionable time.

Coaches, send a message to your team, a serious message. Talk specifically about alcohol and social drug use. Confront it. That's part of your job now days. It's not just X's and O's. Young athletes are making decisions, and those decisions are going to affect how successful you are, how successful they are, and later in life, what direction their life swings.

Coaches that use LOA are vigilant coaches. They don't leave this up to somebody else. They confront it, they educate, and they're willing to do what it takes to keep their team from being involved in alcohol and other drugs.

Advice to Parents

Think of the investment you've made already in your young athlete's life—money, time, energy, trips, going and watching all those competitions, games. Equipment alone, it's astonishing the investment today's athletes require financially. Think about the dreams and aspirations you have for your child. We all want to see our children be successful. All these positives you and other adults provide can easily be undone by one negative if it's pot and alcohol. So many athletes never see their full potential, and a lot of times, it's because no one was talking to them about alcohol and other drugs.

As an adult, be the vigilant parent. Be the parent who's willing to talk about this and discuss it. With LOA, we try to get parents and student athletes to get together once a year at a mandatory seasonal meeting to discuss these kinds of topics. We have programs now for nutrition, sleep, training effect, and recovery. There are so many different aspects of a parent's job now to be a parent of a student athlete, and LOA is there to help.

We know things we never knew. It's not just the coach who's sending that message; it's also the parent of student athletes. And if we can educate the parents of student athletes, they will have a much more vigilant role in keeping young people on the right track.

I think we have too many parents that tell a young person one thing then do something else that doesn't model it. It shocks me to go to sports banquets and see all these young athletes dressed up in dresses, suits, and ties, and there's alcohol everywhere. It can't be that way. We've had state associations that have adopted LOA's ban on alcohol at any gathering that has anything to do with youth.

It's not going to be at a banquet, at an officials meeting, at any venue where kids are playing. I applaud that. If you can't give up alcohol for one night to go watch your kids compete, you begin to see how big the problem is in our society.

Of course, as an adult, that's your right and privilege if you're old enough to partake. But you need to be a positive role model. Kids certainly have enough negative models: their shows, movies popular with them, Youtube, the internet. There's a lot out there that leads them to believe drinking and drugging is part of growing up. Some even think this is part of being a student athlete. We've seen this in some of the programs that we've done documentaries on. So to counter all that negative stuff out there, parents and coaches need to work hard at being good role models.

Another thing for adults: if you want your athletic programs to be successful, you need to

Jim Priest & John Underwood

support what's in the best interest of children. Even beyond sport, I see adults today basing decisions on what's in their best interest rather than saying this is in the best interest of children. Some people are polarizing towns over athletic decisions. Same thing with school differences. If your whole team goes out and gets drunk, gets suspended, and you have a crucial playoff game, it's going to split your team and your town down the middle nowadays. And realistically, that's because we live in such a value conflicted society

Cultural changes begin with lifestyle changes. The cultural changes that are needed in our society are lifestyle changes. Not just in an individual, in groups of individuals where people come together and say there's a better way of doing this than we've been doing it. The power of being in a group of young people on a team is one of the most powerful peer associations known. And I think that we've started something that you'll look back in a few years from now and realize that this is something that's long overdue.

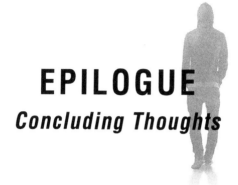

EPILOGUE
Concluding Thoughts

Jim Priest speaks

There are days Reggie and I ask each other, "How long are we going to keep doing this?" It's usually on days we are discouraged and, frankly, it's easy to get discouraged. Every day's newspaper brings more bad news about alcohol and drug use. Crimes fueled by it. Families torn apart by it. Private and public sector leaders failing to do something about it. We often wonder if anyone is paying attention. Is there anyone willing to put some skin in the game and contribute significant energy and financial resources to prevention education in an effort to head off addiction? Some days we really wonder. But mostly we believe change can take place.

We take encouragement from what's happened with smoking. Fifty years ago, smoking was cool. Many people did it. There was no such thing as Surgeon General warnings or "smoke free" environments. But we've changed our culture, and our health is better for it.

Seat belt usage is another great example. When Reggie and I were kids and driving around town with our mothers, our parents thought it was sufficient if they stuck out their arms in front of us when the car came to a sudden stop. There were no such things as seat belts in the back seats or child safety restraints. Now seat belts are a way of life, and no one thinks twice about buckling up.

Think about AIDs. Once it was the dreaded disease that we thought only affected homosexuals. Then Magic Johnson gave the disease a famous face. Millions have been raised for AIDS research, and it is no longer considered a "death sentence." Public education and awareness has made a huge difference.

Another inspiring example is what's happened in the area of breast cancer. Not so long ago, people would speak of breast cancer in hushed tones, like it was something to be embarrassed about. No one spoke the words out loud, and there was no national campaign to raise money and end breast cancer. Then the Susan G. Koman Foundation came along, and the culture began to change. Walks were organized. Talks were conducted. Now, burly Major League Baseball players carry pink bats to honor breast cancer awareness. Reg and I are wondering if we could get MLB players to carry bats to fight addiction and promote prevention of substance abuse.

That's what needs to happen in the arena of substance abuse. We need to take lessons from smoking and seat belts and AIDS and breast cancer. We need to change the culture the same way we have in those areas. It can be done. But we have to make the personal and public decisions to make a difference in how we handle alcohol and other drugs in our individual lives, and how we fund addiction prevention, education and treatment. For too long we have treated addiction only as a crime, instead of recognizing it as a disease that needs treatment, just like hypertension or diabetes.

But we at FATE cannot do this alone. When we send out requests for support we often get responses like this:

> "Great organization but we are not able to participate at this time. I wish you well. "

> "Great cause! Unfortunately, we haven't been able to take on any new commitments for several years. Good luck!"

> "After reviewing your information, we must decline. I applaud your work to address this problem in our state. It must be very rewarding."

These are just a few of the common responses we receive on a weekly basis at FATE. If it is true that "success has many fathers, but failure is an orphan," the same can be said for the fight against addiction. While most—if not all—of us are affected by addiction, few organizations and individuals are willing to join the fight.

At this moment in history, government funding for substance abuse prevention is drying up. While many private foundations are limiting their giving to organizations that meet "basic human needs", like food and shelter, we are hard pressed to find anyone willing to invest in smart, effective solutions designed to take on addiction head-on.

We hope after reading this book you will have the courage to join the FATE team by committing a portion of your time, money and resources to helping us bring an end to this pandemic. We need your help.

So the question we leave you with is the one we started with: What's YOUR fate? What will you decide to do about your use of alcohol and other drugs? What will you do in your circle of influence beginning with the people around your dining room table? What will you do to change the culture in our state and our nation? Here are a few ideas to get you started:

- Examine your own use of alcohol and other drugs. Be brutally honest with yourself. Do you sometimes drink too much? Do you use prescription drugs in an unintended way? When you are honest with yourself, do you suspect you may have a problem? If so, talk to your personal physician or someone who can help you address the issue. If you don't know who to call, contact FATE.

- Look at the people you know best: family, close friends, people you work with? Do any of them have a problem with alcohol or other drugs? Most of us are reluctant to speak to another person about this issue for fear of disrupting the relationship, but think of it this way: you would warn them if their house were on fire, wouldn't you? Sometimes people are reluctant to confront because they don't have enough information. That's where FATE can help. Consult our website or contact us. Then carefully consider talking to this person. Be diplomatic and non judgmental and tell them your observations. Volunteer to assist them in getting help. You may be saving their life.

- Support "prevention education" efforts in your community. Especially, but not only with young people. Organizations like FATE need volunteers and money. State agencies like the Department of Mental Health and Substance Abuse Services need you to voice your support by contacting your legislative representatives and encouraging them to increase funding. Don't sit on your good intentions. Take action.

- If you are involved in a business or corporation, consider what you can do with your employees to prevent substance abuse. You can present prevention education classes during the lunch hour. You can make sure your policies about alcohol and drug testing are thoughtful. You can review your insurance polices to determine whether they properly cover mental health and substance abuse treatment. Be proactive rather than reactive.

Every person has a choice and every person has a decision to make about their fate. To change the culture, we have to change minds and hearts, and that begins with individuals. We hope you'll step out and speak up. We hope you'll reject the stigma associated with addiction. We hope you'll recognize addiction as a disease, not a character defect. Most of all, we hope you'll choose your fate wisely.

That's why we ask, wherever we go: What's YOUR fate?

For more information go to *www.fate.org* and *www.okloa.org*

CONTACT US | VOLUNTEER | DONATE
What's *Your* Fate? | www.fate.org

FATE
ACKNOWLEDGEMENTS

It's hard to believe that it has been over ten years since Brandon left this world. Much has happened since then. For one thing, I can hardly remember who I was back then. I know that I am a different man today.

This book is something that I often thought about but kept putting off. I wanted to tell Brandon's story for the purpose of trying to save other kids from suffering the same fate. However, the years went by, and I am sure that but for Jim Priest, this story would never have been put in writing. For that labor of love, I cannot thank my dear friend Jim enough.

Also, after Brandon died, I was in bad shape. I don't think I would have made it but for my wife Rachelle. The comfort, compassion and counsel she gave me enabled me to put out that fire and decide to live again. I am eternally grateful to Rachelle for loving me through the worst crisis I have ever faced.

I am grateful to my friends Mike Hinkle and Bob Hunter who dragged me to Africa after Brandon died and showed me the devastation suffered by the children of Uganda and encouraged me to help. Working for the children of Uganda helped give me a reason to live after Brandon's death.

I also want to thank two of my inspirations, Sister Rosemary Nyrumbe from Uganda, a true hero, and my friend Bob Goff. Any lawyer who is brave enough to prosecute murderous Witch Doctors in Northern Uganda has to be a hero, and that label certainly fits Bob.

I would also like to thank my kids, all of whom are so patient and understanding. They not only lived through this nightmare of their own, but they had to put up with me taking on the lifelong task of fighting addiction and substance abuse. To Crissy, Jonathon, Dylan and Hannah, thanks for putting up with my obsession! I love you all!

To Robert Newman, my brother in law, I owe an eternal debt of gratitude. He and Rachelle came up with the idea of starting the Whitten Newman Family Foundation, which led to the creation of FATE and other charitable foundations. Robert also faced his demons, having been in a double fatality auto accident in which he was severely injured that arose from a "keg party" hosted by a parent to celebrate his high school graduation. Robert routinely does what most people wouldn't, relive his nightmare, and has helped me speak to numerous schools and thousands of kids, telling his story along with mine.

To one of my dear friends since high school, John Hargrave, I love you, man! I couldn't have made it this far without you!

I also want to thank my dear friends John Newman, James Newman and Dr. Kent Smith for their support, friendship and camaraderie. Brandon Whitten was part Native American, and these friends, along with Brandon's old football buddy, Jeff Hargrave, helped me form the Native Explorers Foundation and ExplorOlogy program. Now young people can learn that science is cool!

I must also thank Jay Mitchel, Bill Horn, Lauren Guhl, and Jeff Hargrave, who put in hundreds of hours helping get FATE started. We couldn't have done it without them!

To my many professional athlete friends, I can't thank you enough! These fellows could have been doing anything they wanted, lying on a beach or making money signing autographs. Instead, they were speaking with me at schools or giving their testimony on video, helping us spread the message that you don't have to do drugs or alcohol to be cool! For this, I am extremely grateful to Roy Williams, Tommie Harris, Curtis Lofton, Mark Clayton, Gerald McCoy,Chris Chamberlain, Billy Bajema, and Charles Howell III.

To the leaders of the Oklahoma Department of Mental Health and Substance Abuse Services, Commissioner Terri White and Assistant Commissioner Steve Buck, thanks for helping us and guiding us on the technical aspects of the disease of substance abuse!

We were novices and knew so little about substance abuse.

I also want to thank my friend Jim Riley who suffered from this disease and successfully battles it every day. Jim has saved thousands of lives through his counseling ministry, and I believe if Brandon had met Jim before he died, Jim would have saved Brandon, too.

I would be remiss if I didn't thank my dear friends Michael Burrage, Noah Roberts, Simone Fulmer, Brandon Nichols and Roxanne Fitzgerald. These friends counseled and supported me on a regular basis for the last decade.

Finally, my greatest thanks to my son and best friend, Brandon Whitten. Many will, unfortunately, remember Brandon only for his last act.

But I know the truth. I remember Brandon coming into the world and forever changing my life and the lives of so many that he touched. Brandon was the most amazing, wonderful and loving child a father could have. As he grew up, he ultimately became the best friend a guy could ever have. Brandon lives on in my heart and in every FATE speech that he and I give to schools around this great State. He lives on in the beauty of the organizations created as a result of his death.

~ *Reggie Whitten*

Reg has pretty well summed up the people I wanted to thank, but I need to add just a few more.

My friend of many years, Reg Whitten, who believed in me and gave me a worthwhile and fulfilling mission to work on.

John Underwood, President of the American Athletic Association, who has been a great friend and unselfish contributor to our Oklahoma Life of An Athlete program.

Kelly Dyer Fry who does a tremendous job as editor of the Oklahoman and fearlessly shares her story, rejecting the stigma, and tirelessly works on the addiction issue.

Murali Krishna and Noah Roberts, FATE board members who have helped brainstorm many ideas for FATE and never ceased to be an encouragement to Reg and to me.

Wes and Lori Lane for being willing to share their story many times, in many venues, with no regard for themselves and high regard for helping others.

Adam Toler and his dad Stan who helped make this project a reality.

To my dear bride of three decades, Diane, and my two encouraging children, Amanda and Spencer. Thanks for believing in me and cheering me forward.

There are many others who, though unnamed here, have contributed to the cause. Forgive us for not mentioning you specifically and thank you for your work.

And to the One for whom nothing is impossible, even the end of addiction, Deo Gratias.

- Jim Priest

APPENDIX

FIGHTING ADDICTION STARTS WITH YOU
BUT
THE FIGHT IS WON
AS A TEAM

You may be a government official,
a parent, or a student
a church, a coach, or a business.
But you're still part of the same team:
our community and our state.

WHAT DOES FATE DO?

FATE is a prevention education organization that educates and motivates Oklahomans to do something about substance abuse. One of our flagship programs is Oklahoma Life of An Athlete, communicating truth about the negative impact of alcohol and drugs on athletic performance to high school and college athletes.

FOR MORE INFORMATION ON THIS PROGRAM GO TO
WWW.OKLOA.ORG

WHEN WE ASK – – – – – – – – – – – – – – –
WHAT'S *YOUR* FATE?
IT'S A CHALLENGE REALLY.

We challenge you to choose your fate
... and the fate of our state.
Take a stand and get in the fight.
Don't look the other way and say "It's not my problem."
Don't give up on the best we can be.
Don't ignore the number one problem ruining lives and our economy:
the abuse of alcohol and other drugs.

SUBSTANCE ABUSE IS

COSTING OUR STATE
$7.2 BILLION

EACH YEAR

THAT'S EQUAL TO $1900 FOR EVERY MAN, WOMAN, AND CHILD IN OKLAHOMA

$$$$$$$$$$

6,530

STUDENTS IN OKLAHOMA'S COLLEGES AND UNIVERSITIES WILL DROP OUT OF SCHOOL BECAUSE OF PROBLEMS RELATED TO ALCOHOL EACH YEAR.

WITH ADDICTION

According to the Oklahoma Department of Mental Health and Substance Abuse Services, alcohol and other drugs cause or contribute to:

85% OF HOMICIDES

80% OF PRISONERS

75% OF DIVORCES

65% OF CHILD ABUSE

WITHOUT ADDICTION
OKLAHOMA EMPLOYERS COULD SAVE
$600 MILLION
A YEAR IN MEDICAL COSTS
GOVERNMENT EXPENDITURES CAN BE REDUCED BY
10.5%

240,000

OKLAHOMANS
(8% OF OUR POPULATION)
ABUSE PRESCRIPTION DRUGS.
OKLAHOMA IS #1
IN THE NATION.

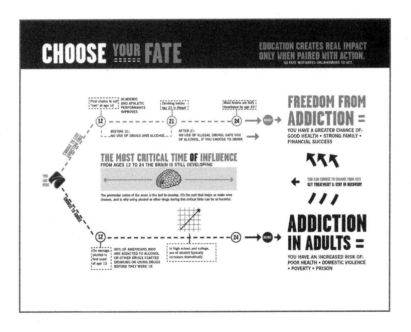

WHAT CAN A BUSINESS DO?

EDUCATE YOUR EMPLOYEES

REMOVE STIGMA

Oklahoma City-based Chesapeake Energy has implemented a companywide program called "Your Life Matters" to help employees cope with drug and alcohol abuse. The company rolled out YLM in 2010 to remove the stigma of chemical dependency and mental health issues.

The program has been well-received. In 2011, there were more than 1,700 phone calls for assistance. A webpage dedicated to the "Your Life Matters" program received 16,000 hits with an employee workforce of more than 12,000. Your business could do something similar.

WHAT CAN A PARENT DO?

EAT MORE MEALS WITH YOUR KIDS

TALK WITH THEM, NOT AT THEM

Staying connected with your children is key to raising healthy, drug-free kids and one of the simplest ways of staying connected is sitting down for family dinner. "Seventeen years of surveying teens shows that the more often children have dinner with their families the less likely they are to smoke, drink or use drugs" says Joseph Califano, founder of the National Center on Addiction and Substance Abuse at Columbia University. Studies show children who eat regular family meals are 50% less likely to abuse alcohol or other drugs.

WHAT CAN A CHURCH DO?

START A PREVENTION EDUCATION MINISTRY

SPIRITUAL LEADERS SHOULD SPEAK OUT

Churches play an important and unique role in preventing addiction and in helping those in recovery. Religious institutions interact with people at critical times: birth, marriage, death, crises. In a survey conducted by The National Center on Addiction and Substance Abuse at Columbia University, 94.4 percent of clergy consider substance abuse and addiction to be important issues that they confront. Yet, at best, only 12.5 percent of priests, ministers and rabbis completed coursework related to substance abuse during their theological studies. Churches need to talk about preventing substance abuse, not just with teens, but with everyone.

FOR MORE IDEAS ABOUT WHAT YOU CAN DO GO TO WWW.FATE.ORG

HOW YOU CAN FIGHT ADDICTION

- COACH / PARENT / STUDENT: Go to www.okloa.org to start Life of An Athlete at your school
- GOVERNMENT: Be aware of and take action on the #1 economic problem facing our state
- BUSINESSES: Take action to keep your workforce informed and substance free
- CHURCHES: Start a prevention and recovery ministry
- GO TO www.fate.org to watch our videos and learn more

Jim Priest is the Executive Director of FATE and brings to the position thirty years of experience in the legal, business and non profit sectors.

Jim is a licensed attorney who practiced law with two leading law firms in Oklahoma City, trying nearly one hundred lawsuits and advising public and private clients as well as corporate organizations and individuals on a wide variety of legal matters. He wrote a column on business ethics for many years in the Journal Record newspaper and was a weekly columnist for the Oklahoman newspaper for ten years writing on family related issues. He has also been a regular guest commentator on News 9 in Oklahoma City.

Jim has a long history of service through the non profit sector, having served as President of the Regional Food Bank of Oklahoma as well as a board member for Habitat for Humanity, the Boy Scouts, Variety Health Center, The Bethany Public School Foundation, Calm Waters as well as Oklahoma City First Church of the Nazarene.

Jim is an ordained deacon in the Church of the Nazarene and an active member of Bethany First Church of the Nazarene where he leads men's groups and teaches Sunday School. He is a co-founder of Marriage Network Oklahoma (www.marriagenetworkok.net) and was a founding member of the Oklahoma Business Ethics Consortium (www.okethics.org). He has regularly appeared on television and before groups speaking and writing a wide variety of topics. Jim is also a member of Leadership Oklahoma and Leadership Oklahoma City.

In 2012 Jim was awarded the "Preventionist of the Year" by the American Athletic Institute (AAI) for his work in creating the program "Oklahoma Life of An Athlete" (www.okloa.org). John Underwood, President of the AAI said ""Jim's total dedication to the OKLOA program has made so much happen in this past year in Oklahoma. The materials they have generated and the professionalism of the program has already started to impact his state," " It is hard to believe how far they have come in such a short time in Oklahoma."

Jim has been married to his wife Diane for 34 years and they have two adult children Amanda and Spencer. Jim was born in Syracuse, New York and graduated from Houghton College and Syracuse University Law School before moving to Oklahoma in 1980.

Reggie Whitten is a successful Oklahoma attorney and founder of FATE (Fighting Addiction Through Education). FATE is an Oklahoma non-profit organization with a mission to educate the public on substance abuse and addiction issues in Oklahoma and to motivate individuals and groups to work to significantly reduce the incidence of substance abuse in the state. A special focus of FATE is preventing substance abuse among young people.

FATE was created to honor the memory of Reggie's son Brandon, an "all-American" kid and football player who became addicted to prescription drugs and alcohol. When Brandon died at age 25 in a motorcycle accident caused by substance abuse, Whitten was devastated. "I was a walking dead man," he explained. "I was just trying to find a reason to live." Giving back to the community and trying to make a difference in the lives of others became his passion.

Central to the mission of FATE is reducing drug and alcohol abuse among young people like Brandon who often consider themselves "bullet proof" and don't believe they can ever become an addict. "I think the worst problem this country has is drug and alcohol addiction," Whitten said. "If we had an act of terrorism that killed as many people, we would be quick to launch a war against our enemy. When we formed FATE, we asked ourselves 'How can we prevent drug and alcohol abuse?'"

Whitten travels around the state on behalf of FATE speaking to groups about the dangers of drug and alcohol abuse – telling and re-telling the story of his son's too-short life and untimely death. "I intend to devote the rest of my life to helping end substance abuse and addiction," he said. "I want to motivate and inspire other people to do something. I hope those who see what we're doing will catch the vision and the passion. Not everyone can make a huge impact, but everyone can be a role model and encourage others to get help."